Accelerating the Spread of Good Practice

Accelerating the Spread of Good Practice

A workbook for health care

Sarah W. Fraser

First published in 2002
by Kingsham Press

Oldbury Complex
Marsh Lane
Easthampnett
Chichester, West Sussex
PO18 OJW
United Kingdom

Typeset in AGaramond

Printed and bound by
MPG Books
Bodmin
Cornwall
United Kingdom

ISBN: 1-904235-02-6

British Library Cataloging in Publication Data
A catalogue record of this book is available from the British Library

Fraser, Sarah.

Acknowledgements

This workbook captures some of the learning gained from working on and supporting improvement programmes in the National Health Service (UK).

Contents

Who should read this book?

Do you wonder why some hospital wards work really well, with lots of evidence that the processes and procedures being carried out are innovative and effective, yet the neighbouring ward staff don't adopt any of them? Why do some General Practitioners adopt new referral guidelines and others don't?

Why do you spend so much time working out, from scratch, how to improve something, yet don't spend any time finding out from your colleagues or from similar organisations how they already do it better?

Are you getting frustrated by your inability to influence change for the better, despite sending out masses of new instructions and guidelines?

You could be a:

- Clinical Governance Lead
- UK National Health Service Policy Lead
- General Manager in an acute hospital
- Manager responsible for commissioning services
- Physician in a Mental Health Unit
- Human Resources Director
- Regional or area performance manager
- Improvement Project Leader

...or anyone involved in the delivery of healthcare services, at any level...

If you are interested in how to spread your good practice, adopt the practice of others, or encourage others to adopt good practices – then this workbook is for you.

Introduction

It's much easier to improve by adapting the systems and processes we already have in place, than to completely replace them. Easier still if you take others' ideas that are already working and adapt them to work even better in your own situation.

The notion of good practice, and then spreading it to others, is culturally and contextually specific. Both the definition of what is good practice, and the idea it should spread, is based on the perceptions, prejudices and policies of individuals, organisations and governments.

In the mid-1800s Britain experienced the Industrial Revolution. This was a period when machinery became the focus for delivering efficiencies. The design and mechanics of most of this machinery depended on the wheel, in its various forms and guises.

During the same period, Japan continued its growth, even after rejecting the wheel. Why was the wheel, often seen as the most basic of man's inventions, not adopted for use by the Japanese? The Japanese labour force was large and relatively cheap. Therefore it was cheaper to use manpower, than to use the wheel or build machines. The use of people as a mechanism for efficiency was also wrapped up in the complexities of Japanese culture.

The imperative **to improve health care** is equally tied up in the culture, politics and context within which it is delivered. A current focus is the search for methods and techniques to spread the pockets of innovative and high quality care that are found throughout the health system.

This means change, and change is traditionally not easy to accomplish. This workbook combines a number of theories, methodologies and concepts, to provide tools and techniques for spreading good practice within health care.

Describing and communicating good practice gathers assistance from communication theory and marketing techniques. Adopting a new practice is akin to learning new skills and attitudes so we also look to adult learning theory as well as social learning processes to help the spread process. We can also learn from behavioural and cognitive processes that are involved in the change process.

These theories, including links to research on the diffusion of innovation and other less explicit concepts and disciplines underpin the tools and techniques described in this workbook.

Copying others

Trying to discover and implement improvements from scratch can take time.

Not all learning comes from self-reflection, analysis and generalisation. Sometimes significant insights can come from investigating how others' have improved their performance. Diverse organisations can prove to be fertile ground for discovering new ways to solve old problems.

Why should you participate in the spread of good practice?

- Patients' and carers' expectations are increasing
- Wide variation in outcomes and processes between practitioners and organisations is no longer acceptable
- New technology is available to improve care and delivery processes
- What worked in the past won't necessarily work in the future
- Shortage of resources, notably time, to invent own solutions
- If your neighbouring colleagues and organisations are improving by copying and re-inventing good practice, why aren't you?

Focus on transferring existing practices

This workbook focuses on the adaptation of known practices into new situations. In many cases where you have identified an area for improvement, there will be another group that will have successfully solved the problem. You will be provided with some tools and techniques to support the spread of existing practices and behaviours to new environments. These are designed to be used alone or as a package. There is no specific 'framework' for spreading good practice – take these techniques and develop your own, taking your local content, context and community into account.

Part 1

Overview

Section 1

The spread process

By the end of this section you will be able to:

- Describe the three key parts of the spread process
- List the main activities in each of the key parts
- Distinguish between the terms 'diffusion' and 'dissemination'

There are three connecting parts to the process of the spread and adoption of good practice:

1 The **SENDING** activity; the communication of information from the source of the good practice or from anyone who wishes to motivate others to adopt new and better practices.
2 The **RECEIVING** activity; the awareness and analysis that takes place in an organisation or with an individual who potentially could adopt the new practice.
3 The **IMPLEMENTING** activity; once the decision to adopt has been made, this activity refers to the actions taken by individuals or organisations to apply the good practice in their local context.

Decisions and actions taken in each of these parts influence each other. Each of these activities needs to be optimised in support of the other, if the spread of good practice is to be enabled and accelerated.

This section describes the spread process and its parts, explaining what happens each step of the way.

Passive or active approach?

Think of fashion. Some behaviours and practices spread passively through social networks without an apparent master plan. Others, such as operational guidelines, are subject to a more active and planned method of spread.

It's useful to distinguish between these two types of spread, and this workbook uses the term 'diffusion' to cover the more passive activity and 'dissemination' to reflect its active partner.

Diffusion

Diffusion is a passive concept. A drop of dye diffuses randomly in a glass of water, in an unintentional and uncontrolled way. Most things can diffuse passively given enough time. For example, the Royal Mint found that after 60 years, bars of gold became contaminated by lead stored alongside.

Diffusion can refer to each of the sending, receiving and implementing activities as well as to the whole of the passive spread process.

Advantages:

1 Its apparent lack of effort in achieving widespread change
2 Its reliance on social networks
3 Its success is dependent on creating and encountering little resistance to change

Disadvantages:

1 The time it takes for a new and innovative practice to be implemented across a wide population. This reflects the difficulty of a haphazard communication process that may fail if the information is a small part of an ever-increasing pool of knowledge.
2 Many potential recipients of the information may lack motivation and incentives to seek out knowledge about the new practice.
3 Bad or undesirable practices diffuse just as easily as good ones
4 It is sometimes difficult for potential adopters to work out whether the information they are receiving is legitimate.

Dissemination

In contrast, dissemination is an active concept. It implies a planned and more controlled approach specifically to the flow of information and it may also apply to the implementation process. Formal dissemination activities are usually targeted at specific audiences and carried out using pre-defined means of communication.

Dissemination tends to refer only to the sending stage of the spread process.

Advantages:

1 If the message is well prepared and the appropriate communication medium is used, then the target audience may be reached effectively
2 The message can be linked to system wide incentives

Disadvantages:

1 If the adopter is not aware of the problems that the communication intends to fix, then the message may be lost in the noise of daily work
2 An overly prescriptive communication can increase awareness to the debit of restricting the implementation of the new practice by not allowing sufficient room for reinvention by adopters
3 A source that is not perceived to be credible by the recipients of the information may weaken the argument for change
4 The focus is on the sending stage of the spread process, often with little support for the receiving and implementing phases.

Diffusion and dissemination are not mutually exclusive. They can be regarded as activities along a continuum; often good ideas start to spread passively and when they gain momentum there starts to be an incentive for a more planned approach.

There is no right or wrong way for good practice to spread. There are faster and slower ways. There are methods that deliver quick fixes that may lack sustainability that may or may not be acceptable.

The key is to try different methods and to learn what works best in your system, by thinking through different approaches and through feedback and measurement of progress.

For example, some general surgeons throughout the National Health Service in England set up small booking systems to provide their patients with a date for their operation as soon as the decision was taken that they needed one. This practice spread amongst surgeons through their social network.

These informal approaches were extended with the introduction of the National Booked Admissions Programme which is an active dissemination process specifically designed to encourage the development and spread of booking systems within and across NHS hospitals.

This planned spread programme, running from 1998 to at least 2002 also provides support for the implementing phase.

Can you identify the diffusion and dissemination stages?

Note down an example in your work place where new practices have been adopted:

(a)   as the result of a passive diffusion process

(b)   as the result of an active dissemination process

If you were responsible for encouraging the spread of better practices in your organisation, what can you learn from the above examples?

How can the process be speeded up?

Despite concerted efforts and the provision of resources and incentives, what appears simple and straightforward often doesn't seem to spread as quickly as you would like.

The aim of this workbook is to help you work through the various stages in the spread and adoption of good practice with the aim of accelerating the process. To achieve this, the three key parts, sending, receiving and implementing, are broken down into smaller segments.

Whilst this method of reducing the whole into the sum of its parts is useful for learning how to make an effective change, you need to be aware than all the segments and parts interrelate and influence each other in complex ways.

The "Spread Acceleration Model", described and drawn below, shows the detail in each of the three parts and how they connect with each other.

This workbook is set out following the flow starting from identifying the type of spread and takes the active dissemination approach. The tools and techniques are also designed to enable the passive diffusion process. Each step described below is detailed in a separate section.

"SPREAD ACCELERATION MODEL" (SAM)

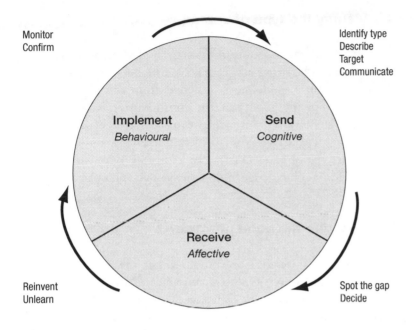

Monitor
Confirm

Identify type
Describe
Target
Communicate

Implement
Behavioural

Send
Cognitive

Receive
Affective

Reinvent
Unlearn

Spot the gap
Decide

(a) What good practice do you know about that you believe would
be of benefit if spread to others?

(b) What good practice would you, personally, like to adopt?

SENDING

1   Identify the type of spread

Not all spread processes are the same. A dissemination strategy with the aim of getting all general practitioners to use the same dyspepsia clinical guideline is different from the dissemination process of applying good practice from industry, such as airline booking systems, and transferring it to the hospital context.

This step encourages you to use a descriptive model to diagnose what type of good practice and spread process you have in mind so that you can design and implement an appropriate strategy.

2   Describe the good practice

Good practice is seldom obvious to either the source or to its potential adopter. A significant amount of research, based on Rogers' (1995) work on the diffusion of innovations, has been carried out on identifying the characteristics of good practice.

You can use these factors, along with others you feel are relevant, to describe good practice if you are the source, or to evaluate it, if you are the potential adopter.

3   Target the potential adopters

Good practice is a valuable product. Potential users need to be helped so that they are aware of its significance and relevance to them. Industry uses tried and tested techniques to segment and cater for different audiences. Research and experience suggests there is a pattern to how adoption occurs.

This step is designed for the disseminator of good practice to develop appropriate plans that build the awareness of the good practice and encourage its adoption.

4   Communicating to make it happen

Ever wondered why the confidential memo accidentally left in the photocopier spread throughout your organisation in a flash, yet the memo on important operational issues appears to be unheard of by most managers, despite a briefing and numerous copies being despatched?

This step introduces the socially constructed nature of our relationships and networks and describes a communications model to make the best use of media and methods.

RECEIVING

5   Matching the opportunity to the gap

As a potential adopter you need to be a good listener and an investigator. You need to pick up the signals being sent in various forms, and if there are none that suit your specific purpose you need to search for examples of good practice.

You could of course develop your own new practices. However, it's seldom efficient to do this from scratch. You will have to change and adapt others' practices when you implement them locally. It's best to start assuming someone somewhere else has already addressed similar issues to yours. What can you learn from them to save time?

It's difficult to know when you might benefit from good practice that others have developed. The problem may be more deep-rooted than the difficulty of finding an appropriate example. In this case, you may need to prepare by analysing your own performance, or that of your organisation, and discovering areas of need and opportunity before you can be open to new ideas and ways.

This step works through how to make the intuitive more explicit and how to prepare for improvement.

6   Deciding whether to adopt or reject

A critical step for you, the adopter, is to decide whether or not you plan to attempt to implement the good practice in your own situation, or not. This is not just the responsibility of the person receiving information about the good practice, but also the disseminator who may be able to help support this decision process.

IMPLEMENTING

7   Re-inventing new ways

Successful implementation occurs when the new ways are matched with and integrated into current systems. The term 're-inventing' is used here to describe the process whereby the good practice is made to fit with the local context.

This section recognises the difficulties of taking a practice or good idea that works in one place, and trying to apply it whole-sale in a different context.

8   Unlearning old ways

This is the flip side of re-invention. The old needs to make way for the new. Running different systems in parallel and partial implementation can detract from the benefits the good practice should be delivering.

Nature's way of renewal and progress, is for things that are no longer relevant, appropriate and useful, to die (or be consumed by something else!). The challenge in this step is to ensure old 'bad' habits are changed.

9   Monitoring progress

Unexpected results can happen from change processes and some people may have a negative perception of the outcome. This step is important in evaluating whether the process has been worth-while, for both the adopter and the person or organisation advo-cating the dissemination process.

PUTTING IT TOGETHER

10 Planning a spread activity

The way in which you go about a spread process will have an impact on its success. This step provides checklists and pointers to ensure you have considered your options and tailored the process to suit the type of spread and its context.

Senge (1999) suggests an organisation's capacity to spread good practice depends on four factors:

- Coaching capacity within the organisation and from the source of the good practice
- Boundaries that are permeable where ideas and dialogue can flow between individuals, teams and departments
- A communications process and information infrastructure
- A culture that sees the spread of good practice as a learning process, where people support each other through the understanding and discovery processes

Further reading
Senge, P. (1999) *The Dance of Change.* Nicholas Brearley, UK

This section on planning spread programmes will explore a number of different methods for constructing programmes intended to scale up the benefits of practices in one unit or organisation across wider systems.

Key points

Diffusion
- Passive spread of practices

Dissemination
- Active and planned flow of information

Sending
- Identify the type of spread
- Describe the good practice
- Target the potential adopters
- Communicating to make it happen

Receiving
- Matching the opportunity to the gap
- Deciding whether to adopt or reject

Implementing
- Reinventing new ways
- Unlearning old ways
- Monitoring progress

Section 2

Building on what you know

By the end of this section you will be able to:

- Define your personal understanding of 'good practice'
- List areas of your own practice, at home or work, that you perceive to be of value
- Provide an example of where you have adopted a practice
- Provide an example of your sluggishness to adopt something others might perceive as innovative and useful

The notion that good ideas and innovative ways of working can spread from one person to another is not new. You are already very good at spreading and adopting good practice; you may just not recognise it.

What can go wrong and why you need to build on what you know

- Rushing into a formal 'spreading good practice' process can be very alienating and overwhelming for all involved, especially if it doesn't recognise the good work and processes already in existence.
- Learning is made more difficult and disconnected if it does not tie into what you already know and do.

It's much easier to adapt what you are already doing, than to try and take on an entirely new way of thinking or working. If you want to find out how to spread good practice, then a good place to start is with what you have already either spread to (or adopted from) others.

What is 'good practice'?

Throughout this workbook you'll be using a variety of methods to determine and describe good practice. As a start, it's useful to reflect on the topic for your own circumstances, both at home and at work.

How would do you recognise good practice? What are the characteristics you would look for? And why?

Note down some examples of your own good practice (remember this can include things you do outside work and at home):

The oil company Chevron has devised four different levels of best practice (O'Dell & Grayson, 1998):

Good idea	Good practice	Local best practice	Industry best practice
Intuitively makes sense but unproven and unsubstantiated	Something that has improved results for the organisation and is substantiated	Proven results, based on thorough analysis, deemed optimum for the organisation	Practice agreed as the best possible, based on detailed benchmarking and analyses
Requires further analysis	Lacks comparative data	May not suit all departments	

In healthcare the number of variables that are constantly adapting and changing makes scientific analysis very difficult and time-consuming. The adoption of potential improvements may be delayed whilst large and often inconclusive studies are conducted to identify 'best' practice.

For the purpose of this workbook, the term 'good practice' is used to cover any substantiated practice that has delivered positive results elsewhere. Will you only be enabling the spread of practices that have undergone rigorous benchmarking or will you be satisfied with sharing good ideas? If you know of a practice that is better than the one you are currently using, do you need a research study to confirm whether you should change your behaviour or not?

What practices have you adopted, or not?

Some techniques, technology and practices you will have adopted more readily than others. Everyone has individual preferences for what they will adopt and the speed at which they'll do so. It's useful for you to start thinking about yours now.

Think about what new practice or piece of technology you have adopted or started to use within the last 12 months. What is it? Why did you adopt its use?

Now figure out a new practice or innovation you have not adopted and never intend to. What is it? Why haven't you adopted it?

You'll discover from these two exercises that you have real examples of what you perceive to be good practice, of practices you have adopted, as well as proof that you are also personally resistant to adopting some new ideas or innovations. This will stand you in good stead for working with those whom you may perceive to be resistant (Fraser, 2000b).

Think about the practice or innovation you have NOT adopted.

You have very rational reasons for this. Do you hear similar sorts of sensible reasons made by others who may not wish to adopt new practices? What do you think about the reasoning of others?

Key points

Good ideas
- Unproven but intuitively makes sense

Good practice
- Substantiated results

Local best practice
- Analysed and agreed as local optimum

Best practice
- Benchmarked best possible practice

Section 3

Why is good practice so difficult to spread?

By the end of this section you will be able to:

- Identify the barriers to the spreading and adoption of good practice
- Describe why they are barriers

This section reviews the problems in spreading good practice, using the steps in the Spread Acceleration Model as a focus.

Why is good practice so difficult to spread?

The process of communicating, receiving and implementing improved practices is complex, especially in health care where so much of the activity is not explicit, but rather intuitive and dependent on the behaviour of individuals.

(a) List one or two difficulties you have experienced in trying to *communicate* good practice to others when your intention was for them to adopt it:

(b)   List one or two hurdles you have experienced when trying to *implement* a new way of working or introduce a new idea into your work place:

Professionals who are perceived by themselves and others as experts in their field may be unwilling to share information. In health care there are a large number of professions, each with their own set of values. These beliefs, prejudices and perceptions may hinder cross-disciplinary transfer of knowledge and know-how. This is an issue for both sending and receiving information.

SENDING

Without those who are trying to motivate others to adopt new ways of working doing so in a way that encourages adoption, the whole process is put at risk.

If you have useful knowledge and experiences about good practice you may not be aware that others might find it beneficial. You tend to see the way things work from your own perspective. Your underlying assumptions may even be invisible to you.

1   Identify the type of spread

By assuming all spread activities and processes are the same, you may

- Increase resistance to change
- Lengthen the time it takes for good practice to diffuse through the system
- Increase the number of potential adopters rejecting the new ways
- Inappropriately increase expectations about success
- Participate in an ineffective and expensive process
- Reduce the opportunities for success

2 Describe the good practice

Not describing or disseminating good practice in a way that enables it to be readily understood and accepted by others may slow down the process.

Presenting detailed solutions on how something should work is more likely to increase resistance to change. One advantage of working through just what the new idea or good practice is about is that it helps you identify the underlying core concepts; the essence of the good practice. Creating awareness, sharing information and enabling the implementation of these concepts is key for an effective and timely spread process.

3 Target the potential adopters

Many centrally co-ordinated dissemination activities are tailored to the management communication process and not geared to the target audience that may be health practitioners. The communication and change process may alienate staff who participate or even leave out some staff who were not aware they should be involved.

4 Communicating to make it happen

Using the wrong media and methods that do not reach the target audience can significantly impact the spread process e.g. using a website when the target population has little access to the Internet.

Traditional communication using formal letters or reports may do little to spread good practice. In most cases a spread strategy will require a number of different methods, at different stages of the process.

Potential adopters may lack the required networks and relationships to enable them to be aware of and believe in the opportunities. They need relationship, based on trust, with a credible source of the good practice.

> A hospital manager attended a conference where a breast surgeon presented referral guidelines for the cancer diagnostic process. She then decided to send these to all the general practitioners that refer directly to her hospital, requesting they be used with immediate effect.
>
> The letter was addressed as 'Dear Colleague' and sent as a formal request for action, accompanied by a file with the details of the guidelines.
>
> *Can you think of 3 reasons why these guidelines were not adopted by the general practitioners?*

RECEIVING

Many potential adopters, both individuals and organisations, lack the 'know-how' and networking to identify opportunities for improvement. They do not know where to discover good practice, or recognise it when it is found, and also lack the skills and capabilities to implement changes.

5 Matching the opportunity to the gap

Highly specialised experts are often not well networked outside of their particular area and may miss opportunities to discover new practices.

As a potential adopter of a new practice you may lack knowledge about your current processes, systems or practices; you may not be aware of the room for improvement. This results from the largely 'intuitive' way that much of healthcare is delivered along with a dearth of proper information upon which improvement decisions can be made.

There is often also a lack of true process benchmarking that goes into more detail than just comparing monitoring figures.

Where health care is delivered through a public organisation, such as the National Health Service, the inherent lack of competition may inhibit the speed of the adoption of improved practices.

Another key issue is one of context. The benefits that accrued to the source of good practice may not be realised in a totally different context.

6 Deciding whether to adopt or reject

A number of factors influence both individuals and organisations at this critical step in the process:

- Unfavourable previous experience of change
- Being a passive recipient of dissemination initiatives may make you sensitive to agreeing to more change
- Credibility of the source
- Benefits not clearly understood
- Lack of support to facilitate the decision process or the change itself
- Inappropriate and inadequate decision process

- Not enough time for reflection
- Not enough relevant information
- Too much detailed information about the solution to be implemented
- Lack of confidence that it will work or others will be interested in the new ways

A new manager in their organisation invited the physiotherapists to a meeting. He presented some guidelines for treating patients presenting with minor strains that were in place where he worked previously. He then described how they would reduce costs by up to 10% and by implementing these guidelines, the physiotherapists would contribute to the organisation's cost reduction programme, especially since the deadline for agreeing change initiatives was the next day.

In what ways did this process inhibit the decision making process of the physiotherapist group?

IMPLEMENTING

7   Re-inventing new ways

Individuals and organisations sometimes display an unwillingness to take on something developed by someone else. This can be exacerbated by central demands to copy others.

Evidence for change processes, including the spreading of good practice, is that some form of 're-invention' is necessary. Perhaps adopting ideas from others may be perceived by some as a failure in their ability to devise the innovation in the first place; competitive commissioning and reward systems can exaggerate this.

Re-inventing and making changes takes time and you may feel it's easier to keep working the current way. You may also perceive that you have insufficient resources, money and people, to deliver the changes. However, it is worth noting that even with resources, change is still difficult to achieve.

8   Unlearning old ways

Part of developing and applying new practices is giving up on the old way. This unlearning process is essential to ensure both the implementation phase as well as the sustainability of the change.

Aspects that will hinder the unlearning and spread process include:

- Lack of belief that the new way will work

- Inability to let go of the comfortable
- Difficulty in working with uncertainty
- Fear of change
- Putting professional tribalism and protectionism ahead of the patient's interests
- Unrealistic expectations such as trying to change the most resistant people first
- Rewarding bad behaviour and using perverse incentives

9 Monitoring progress

Lack of follow up and evaluation hinders the continuity of making improvements. Without feedback it is difficult for individuals and organisations to confirm whether the decision to adopt was the right one. This may have an impact on future decision-making.

PUTTING IT TOGETHER

10 Planning a spread activity

Spreading good practice is a process where the 'how' matters. Difficulties occur and the speed of change is affected when:

- There is a lack of clarity about the good practice or intention of the spread programme
- There is a lack of ownership, or lack of clarity around ownership, for steps in the spread process
- A lack of leadership at the local level of adoption creates inertia
- You misunderstand your role; as an individual or an organisation. You need to know exactly who is the source of good practice, and from where can a potential adopter learn more about it
- The timing is wrong or inappropriate
- There is a lack of incentives
- Unrealistic expectations (e.g. trying to do it in 6 months when the pilot project took 2 years and then getting disillusioned when results are not apparent in 6 months)
- There is a lack of capability to carry out the new practices; lack of skills and equipment
- The organisational structure and arrangements are incompatible with what is being asked

Summary

There is no quick fix or easy way to overcome the difficulties and barriers you will encounter at each stage of the process. The forthcoming sections of this workbook will provide you with guidance and advice on how best to tackle them.

Before embarking on the journey of 'spread', you first need to work out your specific role in the spread process. This is covered in the next section.

Further reading
Robbins, H and Finley, M
(1998) *Why Change
Doesn't Work*, Orion, UK

Key points

BARRIERS
Sending
- Assuming all types of good practice and spread processes are the same
- Not describing the practice in a way that facilitates understanding
- Not targeting communication to the audience
- Using inappropriate and ineffective methods of communication

Receiving
- Current performance is not made explicit
- Not recognising potential benefits
- An ineffective decision making process

Implementing
- Insufficient commitment, time and resources
- Inability to let go of the past
- Poor feedback and monitoring processes

Section 4

Working out your role

By the end of this section you will be able to:

- Distinguish between the 'source' and the 'motivator' roles
- Describe your role in the context of your specific aims for spreading good practice
- Explain the differences between the motivator and the source roles

Different people have different roles to play in the spread and adoption of good practice. It's useful at the start of any spread initiative you might be involved in to work out which role you are playing. It's quite possible for you to have a number of different roles in these sorts of activities at any one time. It is, however, key that you are able to differentiate between the roles and to behave appropriately if your intention is to *accelerate* the spread of good practice.

This section describes the different roles for the *adopter*, the *source* and the *motivator* in the spread of good practice.

Identify an example of good practice you would like to disseminate.

Who is the originator of this example?

Who are the potential adopters?

The adopter

Any individual, team or organisation that has the potential to improve the delivery of healthcare by changing their current practice, using the ideas and experiences of others, is a potential adopter.

For an organisation or a team to adopt a new practice, it will need commitment and ownership from the leader so that the changes are implemented in the best possible way.

It's usually much easier for one individual to take on new ways of working from another, especially if there are no major resource implications.

The source

You are the source of the good practice if you can identify that you are the originator of the particular way of working. As you are unlikely to have patented your activity it may be difficult to establish full ownership. That's not what matters here. What you are interested in is distinguishing yourself as an example of the practice. To be a source, the identified practice must be currently in operation.

There are a number of difficulties in identifying the real source of good practice. You may be behaving in a way that is without doubt recognised by your colleagues as good practice, yet you can't see it, as it is implicit in the way you work.

The motivator

If you are not the primary source of the good practice, but you are trying to encourage others to adopt it, then you are the 'motivator'.

This is a type of source, but the role is quite different.

You are an agent for change and you may have different reasons for encouraging potential adopters than they may have for taking on the new ways of working.

You are the Director of Human Resources at a large acute hospital. Following a review of sickness absence, you work with colleagues and clinical leads to develop a policy and action plan to reduce the average time off work per sickness event. This was implemented and the results indicate a significant improvement.

Your Regional Office has identified this policy as a '*source*' of good practice and nominated you and your organisation, as the source, for 'Beacon' status. The National Beacon Programme means you are provided with funding to help you share your work with others. You were surprised as you did not see this as something very special; you were just doing your job.

The regional office nominated you as they would like other trusts ('*adopters*') to adopt similar policies and practices to reduce their sickness absence rates. In this case they are taking on the '*motivator*' role.

It's equally important to separate this role from the adopter as from the source. It may be tempting for you, e.g. Health Authority, Regional Office or an Action Team, to issue guidance on what you perceive to be best practice and then make the assumption your part in the process is complete. This action is only a substitute for real change. Unless the potential adopters have received the message positively and implemented its recommendations in a way that fits their circumstances, patient care still has not had the chance to improve.

List three examples where you have recently observed an individual or an organisation acting the part of the motivator.

1.

2.

3.

Summary of the roles involved in spreading good practice

	Source	Adopter	Motivator
Main role	**Demonstrate**	**Implement**	**Connect**
	SENDING	RECEIVING	SENDING & RECEIVING
	Provide information on the good practice	• Assess current situation • Increase awareness of good practice	Encourage others to share and adopt practices that improve the delivery of health care
	e.g. an individual, team, department or organisation who has developed and implemented good practice	IMPLEMENTING • apply improved working practices	Help connect the source and adopter
		e.g. an individual, team, department or organisation who can potentially improve practices by transferring the ways of working from the source to their own situation	*e.g. Manager, Health Authority, Commissioning agent, Regional Office, Clinical Governance lead*
Secondary role	**Support**	**Engage**	**Enable**
	Provide support, information and advice to the adopter	Monitor and feedback experiences of change to others interested in adopting similar practices	Enable the wider environment that encourages and supports the sharing of information and knowledge; includes provision of resources.

The source, motivator and the adopter can operate at two different levels, the **individual** and **organisational** (Fraser, 2000a) (see opposite).

Why is it necessary to distinguish between these roles?

The spread process is a complex one. When you are planning a spread programme it's important to work out who will be doing what part of the process and why. Identifying roles, their types and the names of the people who will be carrying them out is an essential part of any dissemination activity.

	Source	Adopter
Individual	A method of identifying patients on warfarin so as to reduce risk of prescribing a contra-indicating drug; developed by a GP *(Individual source)*	• Another GP, within the same practice, PCG or any other group who wishes to adopt the same ideas in the use of warfarin treatment. *(Individual adopter from individual source)* • Another GP starts to use breast cancer referral protocol issued by the National Cancer Action Team *(Individual adopter from organisational motivator)*
Organisational	• A hospital that has developed and implemented a sickness policy that has reduced absence by 40%. *(Organisational source)* • A Regional Office, Health Authority or National Action Team that has produced a clinical guideline that it wishes to spread *(Organisational motivator)*	• A hospital or primary care practice adopts the breast cancer referral protocol issued by the Cancer Action Team *(Organisational adopter from organisational motivator)* • A neighbouring hospital adopts the sickness policy. *(Organisational adopter from Organisational source)* • A PCG adopts the warfarin procedure from the single GP who is possibly from outside the PCG. *(Organisational adopter from an individual source)*

Different needs, different behaviours

Without the source being identified and encouraged to communicate good practice, potential adopters would be left having to invent from scratch, to make improvements. This means it will take longer to deliver improvements to the patient.

The adopters are in a recipient role and this requires quite different behaviours than the more proactive 'sending' role of the source. Adopters need to have access to the primary source to be assured of its credibility and to help the re-invention process. If you are the adopter it is helpful for you to be able to know that the good practice the motivator is disseminating is actually in place somewhere else. You may like to contact the source and discuss how they implemented the changes. This is an important part in reducing your resistance to change.

The difference between the motivator and source roles is key. Motivators have multiple roles in working with a specific area of good practice; in disseminating information and monitoring progress, and also in enabling the wider environmental cultural changes and structural support.

Many large spread programmes are designed and implemented by people in the motivator role, and it's important for them to find ways to bring the sources of good practice into the process.

Provide an example where you are the source, the adopter or the motivator in the process of spreading good practice.

Source:

Adopter:

Motivator:

This section has helped you identify your role in the spread process. The next section will assist you in identifying the different types of spread.

Summary

Checklist – Am I the person who...?

The adopter
- ❑ ...will be implementing the new practice and working in a different way?
- ❑ ...will be directly impacted by the change?

The source
- ❑ ...developed the good practice?
- ❑ ...currently demonstrates this practice in my day to day role?
- ❑ ...can explain the improved process to others?
- ❑ ...shows others how it works?

The motivator
- ❑ ...is encouraging others to adopt the good practices?
- ❑ ...is responsible for enabling the right environment for good practice to spread from one person or organisation to another?

Part 2

Sending

Section 5

Identifying the type of spread

By the end of this section you will be able to:

- Distinguish between four different types of spread process
- Describe the differences and why they are important
- Diagnose which process applies to your specific example

Different types of spread have different implications for the process and if your aim is to accelerate the improvement by rapid implementation of good practice, then everything that can reduce resistance to change needs to be taken into account. Paying attention to the spread types can reduce resistance.

Before designing a programme where the intention is to spread good practice from one individual or group to different individuals and groups, it is useful to work out what type of spread you are planning to achieve. This section will describe four different ways in which good practice can be spread, and highlights the implications for roles, methods of dissemination and implementation as well as other special considerations.

The four approaches are:

1 **Scatter**
Where one simple behaviour or practice is intended to be disseminated to and adopted by very many people.
A guideline for the management of patients with asthma that is to be implemented by all general practitioners and hospital physicians in a health system.

2 **Switch**
The concept from a good practice that operates outside your context, to be implemented in your local context.
The concept behind airline booking systems that the user agrees

their date of travel with the agent can be transferred to hospitals where patients can agree the date for their treatment as soon as a decision has been made for them to be admitted.

3 **Share**

This enables the sharing of wealth within an organisation by copying practices in one division, unit or group, to others throughout the organisation.

*A lung cancer one-stop diagnostic clinic modelled on the same concepts as a gynaecological diagnostic clinic that exists in the **same** organisation.*

4 **Stretch**

Where good practice in a pathway of care is expanded within the organisation, across divisional boundaries as well as across organisational boundaries.

The practice of putting the patient first and designing services around the patients' needs that has been implemented effectively in a colorectal cancer diagnostic clinic, can be expanded to cover the awareness and prevention of cancer right through to the ways in which operating theatres and administration work – all centred around the patient suspected and diagnosed of having colorectal cancer. This type of spread crosses many organisational boundaries.

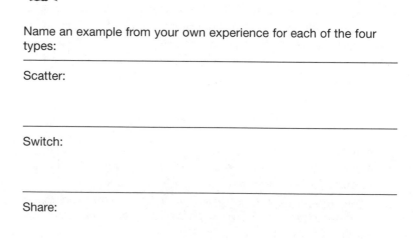

Name an example from your own experience for each of the four types:

Scatter:

Switch:

Share:

Stretch:

How do the source, motivator and adopter roles differ in each approach?

	Scatter	Switch	Share	Stretch
Source	Characterised by a single source. Often one good practice in one location being done by one person or team.	Someone or some group from a different context, industry sector, or environment. Usually distant and different from the potential adopters in may ways.	Individuals and teams who have implemented a new way of working within an organisation.	Usually a single pocket of good practice wishing to expand the same practice to new areas along the patient pathway.
Motivator	Usually a local, regional or central management person who has responsibility for the specific area in which the good practice is to be implemented	Anyone who has encountered an example of good practice in another context and can see how the concept can be replicated in their own context. These people are often from regional or central management functions	The leaders and managers within an organisation.	Specifically clinical leaders within and across organisations, but can also include other managers. Crucially, this type crosses many organisational and professional boundaries and needs leadership support.
Adopters	Significant number. They will usually be the same target population as the source (i.e. if it's a midwife doing the good practice, then it's all similar midwives who are potential adopters).	Often characterised by a pilot phase to test feasibility in the new environment, after which the practice can be spread to others more easily. As this approach requires a significant re-invention process in the new context, the adopters are often more innovative than their colleagues.	Staff within the same organisation, although they may work in very different areas to the source.	Have a similar focus and common ground (patient or disease pathway) with the source. They will be in a number of different organisations.

When developing a spread programme there are some additional factors to consider when choosing an approach. Each of the scatter, switch, share and stretch types has its own advantages and disadvantages with regards deployment and implementation. These are listed below.

	Scatter	**Switch**	**Share**	**Stretch**
Time taken to decide to adopt	If adopters are aware the new idea or practice can fix a problem then this helps a speedy decision process.	Depends very much on the extent of change required. An individual can decide to set up and implement a pilot very quickly if no extra resources required.	Leader of the organisations may decide to implement the good practice across other departments but it may take longer for practitioners to implement the changes	As this crosses many organisational and professional boundaries, the decision making process is often convoluted and slow.
Time taken to implement	Can be quick to disseminate and communicate but then often slow in implementation unless adopters are • very willing to change • the practice is very simple to implement • incentives are good	Often high resistance and could be long time if not pump primed and tested in the new environment to prove the transfer can be made effectively	Slower to implement as departments may be very different. Good networking and incentives may help.	Helpful if personal networks are good. Tends to take a long time.
Reinvention	Not much expected, and it is this that often causes the resistance to change	Quite difficult, so a pilot programme will help. Higher risks overall and the use of unfamiliar language and terms may create resistance.	Will be more than expected, as departments within one organisation will still be quite different in role, function and culture.	Could be significant as each individual and organisation will need to make coherent changes
When to deploy	Wide spread implementation is required and the change is relatively simple to introduce	Searching for radical breakthroughs	Seeking organisational optimisation and benefits	Optimising and improving patient or disease process across organisational boundaries

(continued)

	Scatter	Switch	Share	Stretch
How to deploy	Disseminate and communicate widely Use appropriate social networks Monitor awareness, decision-making processes and impact of implementation.	Pilot first, evaluate and fine-tune. Then communicate to raise awareness of success.	Communicate, network, and connect. Provide incentives. Use project management methods. Gain maximum impact when ideas are shared rather than held by a few people	Communicate, network, and connect Boundaries can inhibit the flow of information and reinforce preconceptions, so enable multi- agency and multi-organisational group meetings. Use project management methods
Special considerations	Needs careful targeting and an appropriate communication process. Often results in lots of *sending*, and not much *receiving* or *implementing*.	Language, meaning and different beliefs and values can be a significant barrier to acceptance by adopters. Use a pilot site to provide evidence of the relative advantage and benefits for the local context. Reinvention is quite difficult.	Make the good practice visible within the organisation. Enable networking across departments, though be aware of close inter-departmental rivalries; it may be easier to adopt practices from outside the organisation, than from within.	Consider the complexity and crossing of boundaries; needs leadership commitment to support all stages of the spread process. Manage expectations.

Think of a recent initiative to spread good practice in your area of work.

How did it progress? Which type of spread do you think it was?

What do you know now that may have helped the adoption process?

Summary

This section has built on your role and helped you identify the different types of spread and highlighted the key issues for each type. The next section will cover how you can best describe good practice so that the process of adoption can be accelerated.

Key points

There are 4 types of spread, each with their own key issues:

1. Scatter
One idea or practice is to be spread to many potential adopters
- Simple to send out messages and yet often the ideas are not received or implemented by potential adopters
- Assumes 'one-size-fits-all' and may not enable sufficient local reinvention
- Assumption from the messenger that their idea is best

2. Switch
An idea or practice from outside the industry sector to healthcare
- Needs testing in the new environment
- Language and examples used may turn off potential adopters

3. Share
Replicate from one part of your organisation to another
- Important to communicate the concepts and not solutions
- Others may perceive the initiating unit or department had special arrangements that enabled the changes to happen and assume they don't have the same opportunities

4. Stretch
Focus on the patient process and copy an idea, expanding its implementation, across many organisational boundaries
- Reaching decisions across organisational boundaries can be complex and time-consuming
- Difficult to maintain ownership and direction of change effort

Section 6

Describing good practice

By the end of this section you will be able to:

- Describe a good practice in a way that supports its adoption by others
- Use characteristics to identify potential barriers and difficulties in the dissemination, communication and implementation process
- Explain the difference between tacit and explicit knowledge
- Identify the concepts underlying the good practice

Many practitioners and managers are not conscious of the way in which they select data, assess choices and make decisions. Therefore, one of the most important activities in the spread process is to make this invisible, tacit knowledge more explicit.

This section will provide you with a technique to describe good practice in a way that will best help potential adopters recognise it and then make the decision on whether to adopt it or not.

The trouble with identifying good practice is that one person will see an activity or behaviour and interpret it in a different way to how another person might. However, there will appear to be very rational reasons for each person's interpretation.

If your objective is to spread what you perceive to be a good practice, then a useful starting point is to describe it in a way that best enables the potential adopters of the practice to understand it. Alternatively, if you are a potential adopter, then you need to be able to analyse the practice being presented and work out its value to you.

A neighbouring primary care practice uses group consultations for supporting patients who have asthma. A team from the practice has presented what they do and how it works, to your organisation.

Each member of your team will have a different view of the potential opportunity:

- The *nurse* might see it as an educational opportunity;

- The *doctor* as a way to get more time with other patients;

- The *practice manager* sees a lot more complication in arranging appointments;

- The *patient representative* sees this as a way to meet others with similar conditions and get practical advice from them.

You are a Nurse Practitioner running a nurse-led clinic for managing patients on insulin. Your patient and outcome results are good and you consider your clinic to be an example of good practice. Your Clinical Governance Lead has asked you to spread your activities to other Practices in the Primary Care Group.

Your first task is to make sure you fully understand what it is you do and how you do it. Then you need to be able to describe it in a way that others will understand it easily.

Your role is to motivate busy people to change the way they do something. It's unlikely this will happen without you carrying out preparatory work.

Further reading
Everett M. Rogers, *The Diffusion of Innovations*, 4th ed, 1995. The Free Press, USA

E. Rogers (1995) has researched and analysed why and how innovations diffuse. One part of his work has been to identify five characteristics of those innovations that appear to diffuse. These, plus three more from Zaltman & Duncan (1977) can be used in a number of ways:

1. To describe your own good practice that helps you make the obvious and intuitive more explicit
2. As a potential adopter, you can evaluate a good practice and use these characteristics to assess its worth and applicability to your own circumstances
3. To highlight the potential barriers to the spread process so that you can manage expectations and put appropriate plans in place to ease the change

Factors to describe good practice

The well-researched factors that need to be taken into account when you are trying to spread good ideas and practices are:

*   Relative advantage
*   Compatibility
*   Complexity
*   Communicability
*   Observability
*   Trialability
*   Reversibility
*   Uncertainty

The next part takes you through each of these factors, examining some of the issues and providing you with exercises to check your understanding.

1 Relative advantage

How clear and how much is this new idea/practice better than the current situation?

If the potential adopters can't see why the idea is an improvement, then why should they adopt it? You need to know what the current status or perform-ance is, what the improved idea or practice delivers, and then be able to explain the benefits.

Potential adopters need to be able to understand the relative advantage in a way that makes sense to them and their own practice.

Suggesting busy people take on more work that doesn't appear to them to have a benefit is a sure-fire way of increasing resistance to change. This fac-tor is critical in the spread process.

A neighbouring hospital has implemented a new information system that sends financial and contracting information directly to the organisations that use its services. You have been asked to provide the same service. However, before you agree you have some questions:

- What's in it for my organisation?
- What benefits will we get?
- How do I know this is better than the way we currently operate?
- Who will see most of the benefits? Does it matter?
- How certain are we that we can get the same results as the other hospital?

What can the hospital that has already implemented the new practices do to help others understand its relative advantages?

Think of an example where you believe you are the *source* of good practice:

How can you demonstrate the advantages of your ideas compared to what others might be doing? What techniques could you use?

Compatibility

How closely does the new idea/practice reflect the beliefs and values of the adopter/s?

Different professions will view the same idea in different ways. You may unwittingly increase resistance to change by using terms and a language style that doesn't endear adopters to new ideas. This is especially true for the switch type of spread where you may be taking an idea from an industry very different to healthcare and then trying to implement it in a new environment.

If you are sending out information to potential adopters you may find it useful to have it checked, or even better, written by someone in the same profession as your target audience. It may not read exactly as you would expect or like, however, it is likely to be more palatable than the version you would have sent out.

> A project manager was trying to gain support for a new system whereby patients would be given dates for their admission to hospital at the time the surgeon made the decision to admit in his outpatient clinic. The idea for this came from the airline industry and the project manager was explaining to the surgeons that there was a lot they could learn from the airline industry and the way they booked and processed customers.
>
> The surgeons were very resistant to change and it turned out later that the main reason was that they didn't want their patients treated like airline passengers. When the project manager started using different language and examples, the surgeons understood better and agreed to the new system.

What language particularly turns you off? List the words and phrases that you prefer not to hear or read about.

Complexity

How easy is it to understand the practice/idea?

Do potential adopters need specialist knowledge before they can understand the good practice? Are there only a few and very specific conditions under which this good practice will work? Can the main ideas be grasped easily and quickly?

The more complex the good practice and the more limitations of its application, the less likely it is to spread.

If you have a multifaceted idea, then a useful way forward is to reduce it to smaller parts and to focus on these areas rather than trying to spread the whole complex system.

> A new procedure for carrying out appendectomies will best be understood by those who do the operation. Experience and knowledge counts.
>
> Some administrative good practices are connected to other complex activities; for example the success of recruitment and retention initiatives in one organisation may be linked to more tacit things such as culture and leadership style. Trying to show how all these link together can become complex and off-putting for potential adopters.

Communicability

How easily can it be shared with others?

If you need to describe your good practice using a detailed manual then many potential adopters may be put off. A short 1-page summary should be sufficient to provide enough information to generate interest and curiosity in potential adopters.

Adopters will have different learning styles; some will prefer written reports, others diagrams, others the opportunity for discussion and debate. It is important that you are able to communicate your ideas and practices in a way that best suits your target audience. A useful step is to find out which method of communication appeals most to your key adopters.

> In some personal research as yet unpublished, the author discovered that many general practitioners preferred two things:
>
> 1　Either short and easy to read communication such as aide memoirs, 1 page flyers, bullet pointed summaries and abstracts.
>
> 2　Face to face communication such as peer review and mentoring.

Write down what methods of communication you use most. To what extent do you think these match the preferences of those who receive your communication?

Observability

How visible is the practice or idea and its results?

If you can't see or recognize the practice, then how can you adopt it? Is what you see enough to help you make up your mind whether to adopt or not? Can you recognise the benefits of the new idea?

> The use of new scanning equipment that works faster and provides high quality photographic output that can be sent to the referring physician sells itself.
>
> In contrast, the group that operates an effective supervision and peer review dialogue process may find it difficult to make this visible to others due to confidentiality. In this case, it can be described either through written documents or video role-plays.

Much of the good practice in healthcare resides in tacit and intuitive behaviours. In addition, although many healthcare organisations are large, the geographic isolation of primary care and the strong departmental divisions in hospitals mean there are few opportunities to 'see' good practice in action if it is not in your area. Your challenge, therefore, is to find ways to make it more easily visible.

Trialability

How easy is it to test the idea?

Those working in healthcare tend to be risk averse; other than in very specific situations, few patients would choose to be part of an experiment. Recognising that practitioners and managers prefer not to take risky actions means you need to find ways of explaining good ideas and practices in ways that they can be tried.

> Changing the whole appointment system at a hospital so patients can be given a date for their surgery at the time the clinical decision is made would entail significant change for the information technology, administrative procedures and consultant diaries.
>
> An approach that helps is one that enables teams to try out what might work best for them, or lets individual consultants test out how they can utilise their current diary system to achieve the same objectives.

Small tests of change are more likely to help the adoption process through increased confidence, than large-scale changes planned in the backroom and then implemented.

Reversability

How easily can the adopter revert to old ways?

This is linked to trialablity for similar reasons. When you buy a car you can test out a variety of options. Once you've purchased the car, unless you have a special arrangement, it is unlikely the dealer will take it back if you then decided that you now prefer one in a different colour!

In the same way, the more a good practice, or better still, a range of good practices and ideas, can be tested out, the more confident adopters will become in making the decision to change.

However, in some cases it helps if the old way can be re-instituted if the new way doesn't work as planned. Some change strategies try to fix the new system in place such that staff can't go back to their old ways of working. Whilst this may work in some cases, many people will see this happening, begrudge it and resist change.

> Replacing a computer program with a new one is a risky business. It is quite appropriate to retain the old system as a backup while the new system is tested and proven to be working properly.

Note down examples of ways you have tested your new ideas to see if they worked for you.

Uncertainty

How certain can the adopter be of positive results from the change?

There are no guarantees of certain results. The fact that one organisation gained benefits does not mean that yours will do the same; you could do even better. There are ways to limit the uncertainty and everyone involved can assist. The source can provide detail about the context in which they made the improvement, motivators can provide incentives and adopters can test and adapt the ideas to best suit their local environment.

A key way to manage uncertainty is to use temporary monitoring arrangements. Gather information on current performance and test whether an improvement is gained as the good practices are implemented. Provide feedback to those involved to help them confirm that their decision to change was the right one. If there are problems in achieving results then spend time discussing whether to carry on as planned, adapt the ideas further or stop.

Using the factors

These factors can be used for more than just describing good practice. They are useful tools for understanding your own practice, evaluating the practices of others and in identifying spread and adoption difficulties.

Describing your own practice

- Can you explain why and how much better this practice is from any other way? Can you prove this with data?
- Can you explain what you do in a style and using language that makes sense to potential adopters? Do you know what might turn them off?
- Does the adopter need special knowledge and experience to understand what you're talking about? If so, can you describe what this needs to be?
- Can potential adopters come and visit you and see the good practice in action? Are there ways you can demonstrate it, other than by having people to visit?
- Can you reduce the practice to smaller parts so adopters can test them? Can you recommend a good place to start that won't take a lot of time and effort?
- Can adopters revert to their old ways after trying out your good practice? What can you share with them that will help them manage their aversion to risk?
- How can you help reduce the uncertainty for the adopter that they will get the same results, or better, than you have?

Evaluating others

When you attend conferences, workshops, visit other places or read an article, you can carry out a swift review to test the feasibility of the presented good practice for your local circumstances.

- Does this fix a problem I am aware of? Do I need to go back and test whether I have a problem in the first place?

- Which parts of the good practice will work in my context and which won't? What will help me decide on this?
- Can I go away and test the ideas out, without requiring further permission from anyone? What ideas are there to start testing?
- Will I need to keep a backup system running or can I make the changes knowing it's not necessary to go back to the old ways?
- How confident am I that I will get similar positive results? What will help me make that decision?

Identifying difficulties

Motivators and those trying to spread good practice can use the factors to assess the possible difficulties that might be encountered during the process.

- Are the benefits clear? Are they expressed in a way that the adopters will recognise?
- Will adopters have sufficient knowledge about their current performance? How can I help them?
- Is the good practice explained in a way that suits the potential adopters? Are there multiple formats to ensure different learning styles are addressed?
- Is the good practice easily observable? In what way can it be described to others? Can the tacit and intuitive actions be better explained?
- Can the good practice be tested in small ways or does it require large scales changes to take place? What are the implications of this?
- Can the good practice be communicated simply and without detailed manuals or long workshops? How can this be achieved?

Tacit and explicit knowledge

If you can use these characteristics as a diagnostic and descriptive tool then the good practice is based on explicit knowledge. This means it is relatively easy to explain and share with others.

On the other hand, tacit knowledge is far more difficult to express. This refers to the implicit thoughts, feelings and actions that occur in carrying out the good practice. For example, your perception of what makes a good doctor may be difficult to articulate. It is more than a person who is competent and able to carry out specified tasks. It's this challenge of making the tacit, explicit, that can help speed up a spread process.

Ways to make tacit knowledge more explicit include:

- Mentoring or shadowing the 'expert' allows you to ask questions and to surface underlying thought processes
- Writing articles and conference papers helps you explain your own undeclared and inferred learning

Key points

Factors to describe good practice
- Relative advantage *(How much better is this idea than the current situation?)*
- Compatibility *(How closely does this idea reflect the values and beliefs of the adopter?)*
- Complexity *(How easy is it to understand the practice?)*
- Communicability *(How easily can it be explained to others?)*
- Observability *(How visible is it?)*
- Trialability *(Can it be tested easily?)*
- Reversibility *(How easily can the adopter revert to old ways?)*
- Uncertainty *(How certain can the adopter be of positive results from the change)*

Section 7

Targeting potential adopters

By the end of this section you will be able to:

- Identify your target audience
- Identify opinion leaders
- Develop a communications strategy based on the characteristics of the potential adopters
- Describe the importance of networks
- Use networks to leverage spread

Targeting the right people with your message so that the adoption of good practice can be accelerated is a three-step process:

1 Identify the main target audience
2 Distinguish, within this audience, those most likely to support a speedy adoption process
3 Assess how you can use formal and informal networks to leverage change

---

Note a good practice you wish to spread from one place or group to another.

Identifying the main category of audience

The target for your communication is the individual, or group of individuals who will be implementing and carrying out the good practice.

It's important to distinguish between the manager or co-ordinator and the person who will actually need to change their way of working.

> You are a Public Health Consultant at a Health Authority, with a remit to lead on Learning Difficulties. Following a national review, a number of key good practices have been identified in the delivery of healthcare for this group.
>
> You have received a pack of information, detailing the sources of the identified good practice and have been asked to disseminate this in your area.
>
> To whom do you send the information or invite to a meeting to discuss it? The managers of the organisations responsible for healthcare, or the doctors and nurses, or other practitioners, involved in delivering the care?

Key questions to assess your audience

Before embarking on a communication or dissemination exercise you need to know more about the potential adopters.

- What practitioner and manager roles are involved in implementing this good practice?
- Which of these perform leadership roles that are relevant to the change process?
- What are their names?
- Are they aware of the need to change? What are the implications of this?
- What are your perceptions of their feelings about this good practice? How might this influence whom else you engage in the spread process?
- What methods of communication will increase awareness and provide information without increasing resistance?

Adopter characteristics

The speed at which new ideas are adopted reflects individuals' different degrees of innovativeness and ability to change. Rogers (1995) suggests some terms that can be used to describe adopters according to the time they take to make the change:

Innovators are a very small category of individuals who enjoy the excitement and interest of trying things out. They are usually the first in their social group to adopt a new behaviour or use of a tool.

Early adopters take some risks but are usually a little more sceptical and take more convincing. These are often opinion leaders who will evaluate ideas carefully and help in adapting them to suit local circumstances. They have effective networking skills.

The **early majority** are those who take a bit longer to make the decision to change, but will usually be ahead of the average.

The **late majority** wait for the bulk of their peers to adopt the new practice before they do the same. Far more sceptical than the others they are also more risk averse.

Those who are last to adopt the changes are called the **laggards**. This group is often viewed negatively by others, however, it's important to note that if you are seen as a laggard by others you will have, in your view, a rational reason for not adopting the proposed changes. Also, some individuals are laggards in one area, whilst being innovators or early adopters in another. They also play an important role in valuing the past and protecting organisational interests that may be adversely impacted by the proposed new practices.

Why are these terms useful?

Whilst they evoke perceptions of stereotypes, if used appropriately in the diagnostic process, they can help you understand the people with whom you are working and help you think where best to start and with whom.

It is important to recognise that people evaluate the drivers for change and go through the stages of change in their own way and at their own time. Some may get to hear about the potential and need for change much later than others; this is particularly true in large and isolated organisations.

The group to target first should always be the early adopters and not the innovators as you might think. Individuals who are usually the first to try things out may be perceived by their colleagues as slightly 'out of the ordinary' and risk takers. Thus whilst these innovators may provide you with some quick wins, they may also be a barrier to the rapid diffusion of good practice. The majority of adopters prefer to copy the behaviour of those who are more pragmatic and credible.

Adopter details check list
Who are the early adopters for this good practice?

Who are the innovators?

What can be learnt from the rational perspective of the laggards?

Organisational categories

Individuals are your most important focus when it comes to defining and understanding your target audience. However, in some cases it is also useful to assess the status of organisations. One useful way is to review how they have acted in the past. Whilst this is no guarantee of future action it does give you a sense of their status and willingness of staff to adopt new working practices.

Rather than use the five categories based on individuals' rate of adoption, you can use two categories (Westphal et al, 1997), recognising there is a grey area in between:

Customisers	Conformers
• Earlier to adopt • Seek to improve technical performance or get a specific efficiency • Like to make the good ideas and practices fit their own way of working • Find ways to get something else out of the change process i.e. they leverage funding to provide more than just the declared benefits • Have efficient networks within and without the organisations	• Later to adopt • Seek social legitimacy • More likely to take on prepared solutions as less interested in major re-invention of good practice • Driven by performance and monitoring measures

If you are developing a programme to spread good practice it is helpful to identify those organisations that prefer, generally, to change only when they need to do so to retain their legitimacy, to continue to be part 'of the pack'. You would avoid your programme being wholly based on this group, and instead focus initially on the 'customisers'.

> The NHS Booked Admissions programme started with pilot groups of Customisers and then after successive waves of new participating organisations, more of the programme started to include those who wanted to join because they felt they should do so, not because they could see any specific technical benefits i.e. they were Conformers.

Working with the customisers and the conformers

	Scatter	Switch	Share	Stretch
Customisers	Dislike fixed 'solutions'; provide them with just enough detail and the concepts and let them re-invent their own solution to achieve similar goals	Best groups to pilot and test out ideas from other sectors. Provide resources and goals and the space for them to operate and innovate.	Allow different parts of the organisation the freedom to re-invent and change what others have achieved. Provide clear goals. Avoid pushing detailed solutions.	It's unlikely all the organisations involved will all be customisers. If they are mostly this type then provide resources, let them challenge and break rules and encourage radical thinking and action. Provide clear goals and aims.
Conformers	Most likely to implement detailed ideas, but only when others have done so. Ensure you provide them with details of who else has adopted the good practice.	Get involved only when the pilots are well tested and others have already customised and adopted the practices.	Use peer pressure within the organisation to help departments to adopt what others in the organisation have done.	Will find it difficult to make radical changes if most organisations involved are conformers. Provide them with information about what others are doing, how they are doing it. Let them meet up with customisers. Explain the gap between current practice and the goals.

List a few organisations who you think are *customisers*, and a few who you perceive to be *conformers*. Knowing this, is there anything you would change in the way you are currently working with them?

Opinion leaders

Both customisers and conformers rely on opinion leaders and their networks to help in the spread and adoption of good practice and one of the key roles of senior managers and service improvement project leaders is to identify and work with local opinion leaders to accelerate the change process.

The concept of the opinion leader in the role of spreading good practice is that this person is usually amongst the first to know about new ideas and that their peers look to them for guidance about whether the innovations should be adopted or not. They have an important role influencing the behaviour of others in the system.

It is worth noting Rogers' innovativeness-needs paradox; namely, the person who most needs the innovation is often the last person to adopt its use. Early adopters often implement new practices even though they are not in the greatest need for the change. Using opinion leaders and early adopters to implement new practices may reflect a 'line of least resistance' approach to change and may not make sufficient impact on overall improvement objectives.

A project to improve the referral process from primary to secondary care for patients suspected of having prostate cancer was not moving anywhere due to a combination of apathy (people not turning up to meetings) and resistance. The project leader noticed that the group tended to go quiet and listen when one person spoke. She spent some time with him outside the meeting, listening to his point of view and sharing hers. After a few weeks, the other clinicians started coming to meetings and discussing how to move the initiative forward. She had discovered an opinion leader for the topic of referrals and prostate cancer – someone whose opinions were respected by his peers.

Characteristics of opinion leaders (Rogers, 1995)

* Higher social status
* More years of formal education
* Greater literacy
* Higher aspirations and ambition
* Tend to belong to larger groups
* Demonstrate empathy, rationality
* Exposed to and uses variety of media
* Greater knowledge of innovation

Ways to identify opinion leaders

1   Ask questions
Project leaders can continually ask questions to discover opinion leaders. Some useful questions are:

* "Who would you turn to for advice on this topic?"
* "You are always learning new ways of doing things. What was the last time you can remember doing something different? Where/from whom did you get the idea?"
* "Before you implement something new, is there a specific person with whom you check it out?"

2   Do an analysis
One method of identifying opinion leaders is to ask the questions above, and specifically relate it to the goals of the intended change, and then map the results on a matrix. Put the initials of each person both at the top and along the side of the matrix. Then mark in each square who most frequently listens to the opinion of whom.

When you total up the results the key opinion leaders will be those with the higher scores i.e. the most people would refer to them for advice and their opinion on a subject.

What can go wrong, when working with opinion leaders?

I thought someone who had lots of local connections and contacts would be an opinion leader but this doesn't seem to have worked out that way?

Individuals who have dense personal networks, lots of tightly woven and inter-related contacts often don't have the contact with external people that would help them spread the word of an innovation or hear about new ideas. Look for individuals who have good local networks, but *also* lots of external contacts and interests.

We did an analysis of opinion leaders but the people in the group disagree with the results.

This is very personal information and some people may not like to have it shared. So check before you do the analysis. Your assessment may highlight someone as an opinion leader that no one would have expected. Alternatively it might indicate that someone who thought they were an opinion leader isn't really seen by their colleagues as one. All of this would need careful facilitation. It's important to think through what you intend to do with the information before you start an analysis.

Just using the term 'opinion leader' seems to cause resistance.

This term is value laden and turns some people off in a negative way. It is sometimes useful to use the term "key influencer" or "role model".

There isn't an opinion leader in the group in which I work.

There will be one somewhere. Look outside the immediate group. To whom are the members of the group talking?

Opinion leadership is a social construct, it is dynamic and constantly changing. It is important not to confuse this informal and shadow system of social connection with the more formal and hierarchical roles in organisations.

Understanding networks

When investigating your target audience you need to consider not only the formal organisational structures, but also the more informal systems that may help your good practice to be adopted by others. Your communication and other plans will need to take networks into account, especially if one of your aims is to *accelerate* spread.

Valente (1999) defines a network as a "pattern of friendship, advice, communication, or support that exists among members of a social system". A core skill of early adopters is networking. The strength of networks is their ability to move around all levels and corners within and beyond an organisation. The ideas and stories they convey around their informal network run in parallel to any management function.

How to recognise an effective networker

- Unlikely part of the hierarchical system
- Respected and seen as credible by peers
- Has influence without authority
- Seeks information from a variety of sources, and passes it on

The informal networking system exists whether you want it to or not. In the same way it can act as a barrier for change, it can also be an ingredient for supporting the implementation of best practice.

List three or four informal networks to which you belong.

These networks are built around the contacts and relationships between individuals. There are five ways to think of them:

a **opinion leadership**

Influential individuals who thoughtfully take on and implement new ideas will talk with others who then copy the behaviour. This is a very effective network in the spreading of ideas. Practitioners who are geographically remote from opinion leaders, e.g. general practitioners or community nurses, will take longer to adopt new practices.

b **group membership**

Groups tend to adopt new ways of working at the same time, largely through peer pressure. Some new practices also require the whole group to change for it to work.

If you are not part of a group you are less likely to become aware of good practice as you may lack the opportunity of discussion with colleagues. You will be a later adopter. For example, a single-handed chest physician in a hospital will probably lack the available day-to-day peer network to be able to pick up new innovations at an early stage.

Your spread plans should take into account what groups are affected by the changes and how you can best target them.

c **personal and network density**

The degree to which your personal network is interconnected can be tight (lots of connections) or loose. A tight network will mean frequent communication around your local system. However, personal networks that are loose and radiate beyond the regular work or personal environment mean you are likely to get information on good practice more quickly.

Motivators can help networks loosen up by providing forums for people to meet, especially those who generally work in very close knit teams or who are geographically remote, like primary care practices.

d **personal network exposure**

The amount of exposure you get to the new practice will influence the speed at which you implement it yourself. If, through your network, you encounter many people talking about it, or in your work practice you keep coming across it, then you are more likely to adopt it as part of your own practice.

If you are trying to encourage the adoption of new ways of working then it helps if you spend time raising awareness and creating discussion and dialogue about the problems and potential solutions. Too much noise and too many conflicting requirements to change will water down the attention given to any specific issue, so clear goals and limited numbers of initiatives also helps.

e   weak ties

Organisational and group structures also influence the speed at which good practice is spread. One of the most important concepts in understanding networks is Granovetter's (1973) "Strength of Weak Ties".

Weak ties are the bridges between one network and another. They shortcut formal communication processes. Without these loose links some unconnected groups would take a long time to hear of new innovations. He gives examples of how most jobs found through personal contact usually involve the 'friend-of-a- friend', someone not initially known by the job seeker.

Opinion leaders are often acting as weak ties across a range of networks and this is one of the reasons for proactively involving them in the spread and adoption process.

What role do you play in bridging unconnected groups? How could you enhance it to benefit the spreading of good practice?

Leveraging informal networks

- identify and support opinion leaders
- enable peer groups to connect (virtually through the internet or in reality through workshops and forums)
- loosen up tight networks
- allow time for explorations and debate
- hold large group interventions (conferences, mass meetings)
- encourage and enable staff to attend and participate in activities outside their organisation
- participate in research projects or any project or pilot scheme that connects a new group of people

Do multi-disciplinary teams adopt practices quicker?

So far, in assessing the target audience we've looked at the characteristics of individuals and organisations, the importance of opinion leadership, networks and ways of thinking about them. Opinion leaders and networks are linked closely with peer and friendship relationships. This next section tests out the impact and influence of multi disciplinary working on the spread and adoption process.

Recent passions (fads) for multi-disciplinary working are no guarantee of success in the spread process. In an attempt to break down the 'silo's' of departments within organisations, multi and inter-disciplinary teams and matrix working has been set up. Whilst this may work well in some circumstances, such as developing innovation, there is evidence to suggest this in fact inhibits the spread of good practice in two ways.

Firstly, you are more likely to adopt an idea from your peers or other colleagues similar to you in status, profession, age and education (Rogers, 1995).

Secondly, the new groups and organisations, with their decentralising and re-engineering focus may have broken up the social networks and tribes within which most professions have traditionally done their work. (Robbins & Finlay, 1998) The changes may be for the better but the loss of social networks may be a barrier. One way to help, is to enable new social networks through informal events and allowing staff the time to get to know new colleagues.

Evidence and experience suggests many doctors will adopt new guidelines and practices when their peers do. Thus, time to discuss and reflect with one's peer group may be a more important factor in the adoption of good practice, than working in a multi-disciplinary team where the same social structures do not exist.

The problem lies between using multi-disciplinary groups to create a tension for change and to facilitate appropriate re-invention and the need to recognise most individuals will only take on a new idea when their peers do. The implications are for a mix of both. Motivators need to design activities and processes that bring groups together where they can work as a multi-disciplinary team and also spend time in their peer groups. A key implication, however, is for communication methods and this will be addressed in the next section.

Key points

Individual characteristics
- innovator
- early adopter
- early majority
- late majority
- laggard

Organisational characteristics
- *customiser* – earlier adopting organisation that prefers to re-invent solutions that provide technical efficiency
- *conformer* – later adopting organisation that follows others to ensure social legitimacy

Network considerations
- opinion leadership
- group membership
- personal and network density
- personal network exposure
- weak ties

Section 8

Communicating to make it happen

By the end of this section you will be able to:

- Develop a communications/dissemination strategy
- Explain barriers to effective communication
- Identify appropriate methods and media
- Match type of spread with relevant communication methods

This section builds on what you already know about how to describe good practice and who you should target. It covers the multi-step communication model that demonstrates how communication happens in social systems; the communications continuum and types of methods ranging from sharing information to shaping behaviour; the benefits and barriers of the different methods; and how to develop a communications strategy.

The challenge is to communicate in a way that facilitates the spread of good practice. This is one of the most critical steps and if done well can influence the whole process for the better. The damage, if done inappropriately, could mean increased resistance to further opportunities for change and improvement.

Communication approaches

In disseminating information you have a number of options open to you:

Approach	Advantages	Disadvantages
Mass communications One message sent to the masses	• reach large audience quickly and cheaply	• largely ignored or distorted by individuals • assumes disseminator has power to influence adopters • assumes adopters are listening and thinking
Two-step managerial Message sent to managerial leaders who then pass it on	• quick and inexpensive • traditional method • filters inappropriate messages • enables local translation	• ineffective if targeted at this group when it is a different group that will adopt proposed changes • local translation works only if rewritten and retargeted to adopters
Two-step opinion leader Message sent to opinion leaders who then pass it on	• opinion leaders are key players; they influence others • more effective in spread process	• need to know who are the opinion leaders • takes more time to plan
Multi-step process Use groups at various stages to develop and disseminate	• higher probability of implementation of new ways of working	• complex • costly • time-consuming

Think about something that you have recently started to do differently. From where did you get the information? Which of the above processes do you think was in action?

Multi-step communication model

The multi-step model is the most useful one to know about in some detail as it also covers the managerial and opinion leader two-step approaches. It provides a framework on how to think about and plan communications.

Multi-step communication model

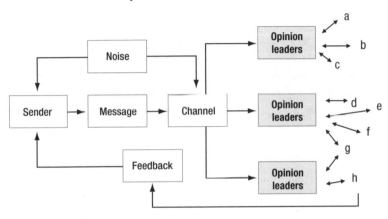

Sender

This is the person or organisation initiating the communication process who can either be the source of good practice, a change agent or another authority keen to reduce variation by encouraging the copying of ideas from one facility to another.

It helps if there is a motivating connection between the sender and the receiver of the message – the opinion leaders and their peers.

A national policy team has produced new guidelines for primary care for treating patients who have diabetes. How do they disseminate these with the intention of all general practitioners adopting their use? Some options include:

National team produces a campaign to raise awareness of the issues and potential for improvement before distributing any information.

Send directly to GPs and to nurses with a covering letter from their Royal Colleges.

Send to health authorities, with guidance that they then hold a brief session for those GP's and nurses they feel are opinion leaders regarding diabetes, and ask the attendees to distribute the guidelines.

Message

Ideas, practices and behaviours are adopted by others when they:

- are better than what currently happens; there is a clear advantage to change
- reflect the beliefs and values of the adopters
- can be understood easily and are visible to others
- can be tested and tried out in a way that is not too risky

Message and method are often confused. For example, guidelines are a method for sharing information, they are printed (or available on the web). The message is the content within them, both explicit and implicit. Lack of clarity about the message and purpose is one of the reasons for adopters not taking on the new ideas.

Noise

Any communication and change process is impacted by noise from within and without the system.

System noise

A key role for anyone encouraging and enabling the spread of good practice is to be able to help potential adopters see a way forward through competing initiatives and activities that divert attention from the spread objectives.
It helps if:

- the message reaches the intended person in a way they prefer, and from whom they prefer
- there is a clear purpose and the action you intend for potential adopters to take is obvious
- the message is simple and the content does not conflict with other messages being received at the same time

Individual noise

The definition of what is good practice is very subjective and information received about it is dependent on personal perceptions. People filter out messages that they see all the time, for example, smokers tend to 'not see' the health warnings on a packet of cigarettes although they may look at the packet many times a day.

Be aware that branding is one of the most significant filters – this is a benefit if you are wanting the customer to choose your product without choice, but has little use where the branding could signal negative feelings (and the communication then being binned, regardless of its content).

Ways to get through the filtering:

- use attention grabbing techniques to raise awareness of the good practice you wish to spread
- send out information in smaller pieces
- offer different ways to access the information e.g. books, internet, workshops, videos
- use branding selectively

Look around you. Can you recognise branding? Look closely at three or four items and note your feelings about each one. What emotions and perceptions does each brand conjure up for you?

What does this tell you about how you should use branding when you are disseminating information? Make some notes here so you'll reduce hindsight bias when you work on your own your communications strategy!

Feedback

Without feedback you'll have little idea whether your communication plan is enabling what you intended. Few companies will put a new product on the market without first checking its suitability, its appeal and carrying out some tests on which message and style will attract the most buyers. This is a discipline that can benefit healthcare, with the potential of reducing the costs of dissemination and increasing adoption. It does require more work by the originating sender of the message and may require alterations and customization of the message for different audiences.

The communication process is as much about awareness as it is about directing implementation. A potential adopter needs to be aware of the possibility to improve and aware of some ideas to solve this identified problem (the good practice) before changing ways of working.

Ways to measure awareness

- Against a baseline, who is now more aware than they were before the communications programme started?
- Are some groups and professions gaining awareness quicker than others? Does this matter?
- Do the opinion leaders know about the new practices? Are their views positive?
- Which of the communications methods (e.g. video, seminar, article) had the most impact in terms of raising awareness?
- Is awareness dropping off or increasing over time?
- Which part of the message or which method seems to have the least impact or create resistance to change?
- What does the pattern of awareness look like? What can we learn from this?

Channel (or method)

Communication implies dialogue. The spread process is more than just sending information to potential adopters. Most spread strategies require multiple methods at different times of the process. A useful framework to use when planning communication activities is the communications continuum.

Sharing information   **Shaping behaviour**

$\longleftarrow\hspace{8cm}\longrightarrow$

General publications	Personal touch	Interactive activities	Public events	Face-to-face
Flyer	Letter	Email	Road shows	One-to-one
Newsletter	Postcard	Telephone	Fairs	Mentoring
Videos	Card	Visits	Conferences	Seconding
Static website		Workshops	Presentations	Shadowing
Manuals		Seminars	Exhibitions	Job swaps
Articles		Training event	Mass meetings	
Guidelines		CD-ROM	Rallies	
Posters		Networks		
Exhibition		Tours		
Reports		Projects		
Benchmarking studies		Audit meetings		
Distance learning				
Briefing				
Bulletins				
Annual report				

Communications continuum

Communication that shapes behaviour is distinguished from the sharing of information by its two-way nature. One-way methods, such as letters and reports, withhold feedback. The recipient is unable to ask questions, to comment or to check understanding. Likewise, the sender is unable to get feedback on whether the message has been received and how people feel about it.

List at least one example of each of the categories in the communications continuum that you have used as a sender or experienced as a receiver of information over the past month.

General information:

Personal touch:

Interactive activities:

Public events:

Face-to-Face:

Which of the above examples had the most impact on you, and why?

Benefits and barriers in the different methods

Each of the methods of communication has it own uses. It's important to use the right one, in combination with others, to achieve your spread objectives. Different areas of good practice will have different target adopters and different circumstances. Each spread process requires its own strategy (see next page).

Different approaches to spread need alternative approaches to communication. There is no right or wrong way to communicate, though some ways are more effective and efficient. The decision on how to match the spread approach with the communication approach will depend on your context as sender or adopter. The issues to be considered are listed below:

	General publications	Personal touch	Interactive activities	Public events	Face-to-face
+	Inexpensive Quick Wide distribution short lead time High frequency	Higher response rate Inexpensive	Good learning process Inter-personal Higher output Feedback Increases awareness Comprehension Retention	Sense of ownership and belonging Explanation Inter-personal Adds credibility Feedback Wide/local coverage Retention	Maximum learning Feedback Increase success Comprehension Retention
—	Don't know whether received or understood Low profile	Need to know names Takes time	Time away from daily work Inaccessible to some Higher production costs	Expensive Inaccessible to some Long lead time Low frequency	Time-consuming Limited in scale and scope

Scatter

The scatter spread approach is about getting a single message to the widest possible audience. The temptation is to carry out mass communication in the hope enough recipients will receive it, understand it and implement the new ideas. However, this is seldom effective, is costly, and adds noise to the system.

You may need to adjust your expectations with regards to the amount of time it will take for the whole audience to receive and implement your message. Once you've accepted it will take longer than you like, you can use the time in new and different ways. For example, consider raising awareness and supporting implementation in geographic pockets. Plan the process in sequential steps according to area. Whilst this may not seem an equitable process, it may achieve greater impact in the longer term.

Switch

Sharing good practice across sectors is risky and difficult. You will already have piloted to see whether it works and will have discovered a new language and way of describing the better practice that makes sense to the adopters in health care.

The NHS National Booked Admissions Programme started with an idea that patients can be booked like airline passengers. The concepts were tested in pilot schemes and then the new health care good practices rolled out across England using a project management framework, with support from experienced project managers.

As these are more likely to be more radical changes they are best explained and explored in participative session where staff can ask questions and be supported in finding ways to make the ideas work in their circumstances. A project rollout approach could be useful, especially if staff from the pilot project support it.

Share

Encouraging departments in your organisation to adopt similar practices demonstrated by colleagues can be a complex process. The advantage of having both the source and potential adopters of good practice within one organisation is that it is easier to manage a formal communication strategy. Of course the informal social system within the organisation will reach outside the boundaries so you may need to find ways to leverage this shadow system and not rely on formal methods.

Identifying and supporting opinion leaders is helpful for the share approach to spread. The credibility of these key influencers and evaluators depends on their accessibility to and variety of information about the topic in hand. You can help opinion leaders be effective by enabling peer-to-peer networking and opportunities for discussion.

Adopters may be sensitive to having their colleagues' solutions thrust upon them so an approach that uses the concepts and ideas about the good practice may be more successful than a specific project-managed rollout method.

Stretch

Spreading good ideas along a pathway of care in a way that crosses many organisational boundaries requires a variety of communication tactics. Strategies to create awareness about the opportunities for change are essential. This means starting with methods designed to share information in manageable pieces, focused on the needs and preferences of potential adopters. You can work within the formal communication structures of the various organisations, however, this type of spread needs the influence of communication external to the involved organisations.

For example, implementing good practice along the whole pathway of care for patients with lung cancer can be supported through articles in journals, Royal College training and development events and by involving the patients, carers and users themselves.

Before moving on to the steps in creating a communication strategy, it's worth a closer look at what can go wrong with communication.

Communication barriers

As a potential adopter of new ideas, what barriers do you think you encounter or create that stop you taking on new ideas?

The matrix on the following page, adapted from Torrington & Hall (1987) lists some of the issues from the perspectives of the different roles in the spread and adoption process.

Your communications strategy needs to take into account:

- The target audience
- Your spread approach
- Possible barriers
- Your specific objectives

	Source	Adopter	Motivator
Barriers in the sending process	• Unaware the message is needed by others • Prejudgement about the message; only see their own view • Prejudgement about the adopters; who they are and what will interest them • Inability to make tacit knowledge explicit		• Inappropriate targeting of adopters • Unaware of conflicting requests for change
Barriers to receiving		• Unaware of the need for change • Previous difficult experiences of change • Needs and anxieties • Beliefs and values • Attitudes and opinions • Expectations • Personal prejudices • Too much noise in the system	
Barriers to understanding	• Complex semantics and jargon • Communication skills • Length of communication • Method of communication	• Semantic problems • Concentration • Listening abilities • Knowledge (too much or too little) • Personal prejudices • Poor receptivity to new ideas	• Use of jargon • Length and method of communica-tion
Barriers to acceptance	• Weak networks and links; not peers of adopters • Personal characteristics • Dissonant behaviour • Attitudes and opinions • Beliefs and values • Unwilling to share relevant information	• Attitudes, opinions and prejudices • Beliefs and values • Receptivity to new ideas • Frame of reference doesn't include new ideas • Personal characteristics • Interpersonal conflict • Status differences; not peers of the source • Previous experience of similar interactions	• Lack of feedback for learning • Weak link with potential adopters
Barriers to action	• Unwilling to provide further information or support	• Memory and retention • Level of acceptance • Flexibility for change of attitudes, behaviour etc • Personal ability to cope with risk and uncertainty	• Lack of feedback • Poor support

Developing the communications strategy

A communication strategy is specific to each good practice that you wish to spread (Fraser 2000a). The process of analysing your target audience, approach and objectives for each programme is important as you can't assume that what worked for one idea, would work in a different context. Your strategy will contain a variety of methods and media aimed at reaching your target audience and supporting the required changes in practice.

This need not be an onerous task and depending on the size of the task in hand, the whole process, from steps 1 to 5 can be outlined in a short meeting of interested parties lasting no more than an hour or so.

Steps to develop communications strategy

Step 1 Identify and agree objectives

Step 2 Analyse the good practice using the factors (in section 6) and identify potential difficulties and barriers the adopters might encounter; analyse the implications for communicating the good practice.
List the key concepts underlying the practice (i.e. not the details of the solution)

Step 3 Identify the target audience of potential adopters

Step 4 Use the "Communication Continuum" to develop a strategy ensuring you have a variety of different methods, and use more than one method at a time.

Step 5 Draft a plan of action including measures for assessing progress and effectiveness of the various communication activities. Ensure frequent reviews and the ability to change the plan, based on feedback.

In this section you have covered some of the most important aspects of spread – communication. You will probably need to do far more of it than you expect and also be quite creative in order to target you potential adopters most effectively.

Key points

Communication approaches
- Mass communication
- Two step managerial
- Two step opinion leader
- Multi-step process

Multi-step communications model
(sender, message, channel, noise, opinion leaders, feedback)

Communications continuum
(general publications, personal touch, interactive activities, public events, face-to-face)

Types of barriers
(in sending, to receiving, to understanding, to acceptance, to action)

Part 3

Receiving

Section 9

Matching the opportunity to the gap

By the end of this section you will be able to:

- Describe the importance of identifying the gap between current and potential performance
- Develop a benchmarking plan
- Identify the opportunities for change

This section emphasises the need to assess the potential for improvement by checking your current performance, assessing the potential for improvement and then working out how best to improve it

The key reason for enabling the adoption of better practice is to make an improvement. To know whether you have made an improvement you need to have an idea about what you are trying to accomplish and details about your starting point, your baseline.

In the diagram below the first bar shows the current level of performance. The second bar is the target. The gap in between is what you need to be working on.

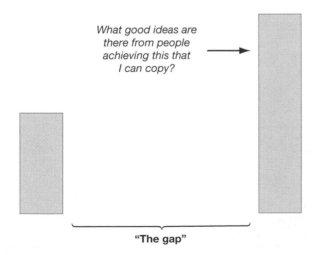

What good ideas are
there from people
achieving this that
I can copy?

"The gap"

You can approach assessing the 'gap' between your current performance and planned improved performance in two different ways:

1 Assess your own performance and make a judgement whether and how much you can improve (**target**)
2 Compare your performance to what others achieve in similar circumstances (**benchmarking**)

Benchmarking is more than gathering results from different individuals, teams or organisations and then making comparisons. It is also about finding out how it is that some people achieve better results.

Both cases require you making an effort to make your current performance explicit (see opposite).

List two or three examples where your practice, service or organisation is benchmarked against other practices, departments or organisations.

(1) Target	(2) Benchmarking
Strengths	**Strengths**
• Can start improving any time, any where and quickly • Can get some results quickly • Fits closely with local circumstances	• Shows the extent to which improvement can be delivered • Provides examples of source of good practices • Can increase stimulus and tension for change
Weaknesses	**Weaknesses**
• Difficult to know whether the baseline is good enough or not • The chosen target could be too little or too much stretch • Can miss opportunities to deliver radical improvements, if others already proven it's possible • Often no stimulus to check own performance	• Resources; cost and time • Comparisons can be argued to be invalid unless samples are sufficiently similar • Focus of attention can become the benchmarking activity and not the improvement activity

Some benchmarking is a quite formal process and is made evident through management reports or participating in a specific benchmarking group. Others are more informal, subjective and qualitative. For the purposes of large scale improvement, it is useful to back up the informal processes with a more formal approach as this will lend credibility to the opportunity facing you and those with whom you work.

Deriving a target

There are no hard and fast rules on how to derive a target. This is an exercise that most managers conduct on an annual basis when they are predicting how throughput and costs will be profiled over the forthcoming year. Targets are just something to aim for and are often very imprecise as they reflect either wild guesses or the desire to fulfil a wider objective e.g. to cut the overall organisational budget by 3% means everyone has to find a way of calculating new, lower targets for the next year.

Quality improvement targets are more complex and you may find yourself compromising on the opportunity to improve because reaching the target seems too difficult, especially if you haven't had the chance to learn about others who have actually achieved the target.

> Monthly reports on the numbers of people waiting for operations in the NHS in England is and example of a formal managerial type of benchmarking. A hospital can see how other similar hospitals are performing.
>
> The key here is to find out more: why do some perform better than others? What happens in their system?

Your current patient satisfaction performance is 72%. With no benchmarking information, would you choose a target of 90% or 100%? Why?

This is a difficult call. Choose 100% and not reach it and your management might accuse you of under performing. Alternatively, choose 90% and patients may complain – is accepting 10% poor service acceptable? If you knew of a number of organisations that regularly achieved 97% would you feel different about this choice?

The target approach, without benchmarking, can lead to meaningless measurement.

Tips for benchmarking

Benchmarking is a sophisticated activity that is a discipline in its own right. There are complex programmes that run over many years evaluating different variables of an organisations' performance. You may be lucky enough to participate in one of these programmes, but if not, you can still carry out a modest exercise to assess your performance against others.

Stage 1: Plan

This can be the lengthiest stage but it is worthwhile ensuring you are carrying out an activity that is appropriately focused. Start by working out what it is that you wish to benchmark. Is it an organisation-wide process (e.g. waiting list management) or service specific (e.g. Endoscopy service).

Who would be useful comparators? It is useful to have more than one and you are best choosing organisations or departments that are similar to yours. For example, if your hospital is a rural district general hospital servicing a population of 400,000 then try and find similar organisations to compare yourself with.

What sort of information will you need to be able to compare against your own processes, who will collect it and how will they do it? Remember you may be asking others to do some work so the more simple and easy you can make the data collection the better. Not all data needs to be quantitative and a visit to the organisation with a brief to capture both tacit and explicit knowledge may be a useful tactic and one that is not too difficult to achieve.

Stage 2: Do

Carry out your plan to compare yourself with other groups and organisations. Remember to ask questions and to gather as much information as possible. If you are assessing equipment and resources, or a specific service, then ask if you can make a video recording.

Stage 3: Review

Set aside time with your team to analyse what you have learnt. Ask yourself questions and explore the opportunities for improvement. Look for the underlying ideas and concepts behind others' good performance. How might these be applied in your own organisation?

Stage 4: Action

Develop a plan for action, building on what you have learnt. Gain support for your proposals and move to the stage of re-inventing new ideas to suit your own context.

Many target based improvement projects seem to start at Stage 4. By now you should recognise the benefits of benchmarking. Although it will take you more time up front, it will enable you to define your objectives more clearly and help you with ideas for change and improvement. It will also help you demonstrate to your stakeholders what you have achieved.

Discovering ideas

Knowing the size of the gap and the extent you need to improve is only the start. You can choose to work entirely within your department or organisation to deliver the improvements. Or you can choose to spend some time learning how others have solved the same issues that you face, and then re-invent those ideas into something that works for you. It is very tempting to start off on your own and you can get going more rapidly and may start to see some small-scale improvements quite quickly. On the other hand, learning from others' experiences is more time-consuming and costly at the start, though you may discover ideas that will save you time and money later on in your improvement process.

It is difficult to learn about others' achievements in a passive way. Yes, you can read about it in articles and papers. However, the best way is to make contact with the individuals involved in the good practice, either by telephone, or even better by a visit. This way you can get an idea of some of the more subtle aspects of the good practice and the process by which it was achieved. You may even find them willing to share with you some of the mistakes they made on the way.

Ask questions

In your search to find ideas on how to bridge the gap in your performance, you will need to ask many questions. Apart from the explicit information like reports, charts, articles and papers, you will also be investigating some of the more tacit and informal knowledge that underlies some of the potential solutions and ideas.

Before any visit or request for information you could sit down with your team and work out the questions you would like answered. A good start is to think about the who, why, where, what, when and how questions. However, there will be other more detailed questions for you to ask those who deliver the service better than you, as well as questions you can ask of yourself and your team.

Checklist of types of questions to ask:

Diagnostic	• Broadly based, aimed to stimulate discussion and understanding about the issue or the good practice from elsewhere.. • Who, why, where, when, what, how
Priority	• What's the most important issue to resolve?
Factual	• To discover the detail behind others' good practice; mostly through gaining explicit information. • More on who, why, where, what, when and how
Hypothetical	• Consider the 'what if' questions. • What if the priorities were changed, additional resources was made available, a new chief executive joined..? • If we were an airline company, what would we do? • Who is doing this better than us now? • What old idea can we resurrect?
Summary	• What can we learn from this example? • What ideas have we copied in the past? • What are the general concepts and ideas underlying the good performance?
Synthesis	• How does this tie in with other improvement initiatives in our organisation

Matching the opportunity to the gap

If you have carried out some benchmarking activities, visited a number of other organisations that seem to have a better performance than you and spent some time discussing the problem with colleagues, then you will find you have many good ideas on how to improve your performance.

Choosing which one to pursue is a judgement call. You know your context, team and organisation better than any outsider. However, your knowledge also includes a number of biases and experiences that may colour this judgement.

It is important at this stage that you just gather the ideas and share them with others, before closing out and deleting any of them as inappropriate or

> The practice manager truly believed that Dr Kadre was unable to change. He had always appeared resistant and she thought there was no way he would participate in the initiative to improve the time it took for patients to access their GP. She didn't include him in the initial plans and activities on the project.
>
> One of the ways of improving access was to use the email system. What the practice manager didn't know was that Dr Kadre's son was a web designer and he took a keen interest in his son's work. It was several months into the project before the Practice Manager realise Dr Kadre had actually taken on the use of email with his patients – without any support or request to do so.

irrelevant. In the next sections we'll look at the process of deciding to adopt or reject ideas and also the process of reinventing them to suit the local circumstances.

Key points

Target
Your own measure based on your own information

Benchmarking
Process by which you gain information about how well your performance stacks up against that of other groups and organisations.

Section 10

Deciding whether to adopt or reject

By the end of this section you will be able to:

- Explain how decisions are made to either adopt or reject good ideas
- Describe the differences between individual and organisational decision-making in the context of spread
- Use the Stages of Change Model to diagnose an approach to support decision making

Adopting ideas from elsewhere is not an automatic process or one that can be managed through a project management system that doesn't pay attention to the subtle and important decision-making processes of individuals and organisations.

This section covers some of the informal and formal issues of the decision making process for individuals and organisations, how you might influence this as well as the implications for the source, adopter and motivator roles.

Recall an occasion where you believe you were resistant to a new initiative and took the decision, either formally or informally, not to implement the proposed new ideas. Now list some of the reasons why:

Deciding to adopt

Whether an individual or an organisation makes the decision to adopt, there are some key factors to consider:

1   The decision is to take a good practice that is in operation elsewhere, and to reinvent it to suit the local circumstances, not to apply the practice "as is". You will encounter less resistance if you take the approach of encouraging the spread of ideas and concepts, and not detailed solutions
2   The decision to adopt is not the same as implementation. For example, the fact that GPs in a PCG agree to use a breast cancer referral form, does not mean they actually use it. The adoption process is effective and useful only when behaviour actually changes.
3   For every opportunity to agree to accept and trial a new practice, there is its corollary – rejection. And rejection helps build a history. The more an individual or group rejects opportunities, the greater the likelihood of their resistance to future changes.
4   The manner in which the ideas are communicated to potential adopters can influence their receptiveness to them, and thus their decision-making process.

In the spread process there are two types of decision-making that can be taken at two levels (see opposite):

Getting going

Information that is disseminated in a way that does not address the target audience, is disconnected from both strategic and operational context and is unclear, will turn off potential adopters very quickly.

Most health practitioners and managers have a significant amount of information to deal with as well as meetings and workshops to attend. You need to start on the premise that there is already the seedling of a 'reject' decision growing in the minds of your potential adopters. This is why it is so important to communicate your message in a constructive and useful way.

The informal and unconscious decision-making stage can also be linked to the pre-contemplation stage of the change model designed by Prochaska & DiClemete (see figure below). At this

	Informal unconscious	**Formal conscious**
Individual	An opinion will form anyway. It is useful to extract what this is and what might influence it by questioning and understanding the adopter's position.	If all aspects of implementing the new ideas are in the control of the adopter, the decision to adopt or reject new ideas can happen quite quickly.
	For example, due to previous bad experiences with new technology, the senior radiologist starts with a prejudice against any proposal for updating the equipment in her department. She isn't aware of this bias.	*For example, the single-handed GP finds it easy to decide whether to adopt the new guidelines for treating patients with diabetes.*
Organisation	The culture of the group as well as its history and current strategic and operational context will influence whether it is aware of or open to implementing good practice.	Can be taken quite quickly by a management team.
	Some individuals in the organisation may adopt better practices regardless of any management decision or co-ordination.	Will take longer to implement, as those who need to make the changes were not involved in the decision-making.
	For example, a rural hospital that has for many years worked in isolation may be so used to solving its own problems without any help that it never considers ideas or options from elsewhere. The same management has been in place for a long time and they no longer notice areas of questionable performance thus don't see the opportunity of good ideas when they do pass their way.	*For example, the board of the new Mental Health Trust may decide that adopting the new guidelines for supporting patients with early onset dementia, along with good practice from a neighbouring organisation, should be adopted immediately.*
		They can make the decision, but it is likely to be a long time before implementation takes place in this newly formed organisation.

stage the individual is unaware of the issues or ideas and you might perceive this as ambivalence, denial or complacency towards what you think is a problem to be resolved.

Working with someone who is at this early stage of change or decision-making is challenging. Your role is to make the current performance explicit in such a way that the person becomes willing to change and adopt new ideas and practices. It helps if you target your efforts on the issues and tension for change rather than to try and push through a solution.

The bed manager in the local acute hospital was unaware (pre-contemplative stage) that the way in which she managed the bed allocation process was not the optimum. She managed to keep the process going through her contacts and knowledge even though this often meant she needed to bypass her own procedures.

The quality improvement manager had recently met a colleague at a neighbouring hospital and learnt how they managed their bed allocation and the benefits of their system. He encouraged the bed managers of the two hospitals to meet and share their information. His bed manager started to become aware that her system was not as good as it could be (contemplative stage). However, she saw many barriers to taking action so didn't do anything about it.

A few months later the quality manager spent some time understanding the barriers and then helping the bed manager see a way her new ideas could be implemented. They drew up a plan and she started to make some small changes (action stage). These worked for a while (maintenance stage) and then there was an outbreak of MRSA on one of the wards and she threw out the new system and went back to her old ways (relapse stage). She was convinced the new system wasn't the right thing to do and was now quite resistant to further change.

The Stages of Change Model
(adapted from Prochaska and DiClemente, 1984)

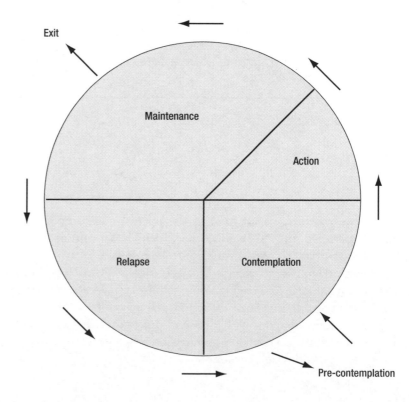

Using the Stages of Change Model to enable the decision making process for individuals

Pre-contemplation

- Increase the tension for change by making the current performance more explicit; through audits, feedback, peer review, benchmarking etc.
- Recognise the individual is at this early stage and don't push new ideas or solutions
- Find ways to hold discussion in a safe and exploratory way i.e. not at meetings where the person may feel threatened or intimidated by others
- Break the issue into manageable pieces and don't push for big decisions until smaller ones have been made. For example, implementing a one-stop clinic doesn't need to happen all at once. The first decision could be to find a way to do two of the diagnostic tests on the same day, on the basis that it reduced the number of journeys to the hospital that the patient needs to make.
- Use a peer group to find ways to influence the person

Contemplation

- Expect dissent and disagreement at this stage; work through the issues and help the potential adopter to overcome the barriers to change that they perceive
- Be an active listener; encourage and support the person and the team to work through their concerns and see how the ideas might best be implemented
- Provide information as requested; be as honest, open and helpful as possible
- Don't push for action until they are ready

Action

- Provide support and help with any additional decision making that may arise
- Expect slippage back and forth between contemplation and action; keep focused on what the decisions are that need to be made to move forward, and provide support accordingly

Maintenance

- The key decision to watch out for here is the one to stop the new practice because it isn't working as expected; ensure feedback on progress at all times
- Check the performance is what was anticipated and help the individuals decide to continue to improve rather than just stop at a point they deem satisfactory. This may mean increasing the tension for change again.
- Sometimes the new practice doesn't work that well and should be stopped; recognise this, provide support, discuss learnings and move on

Relapse

- Check that your understanding of relapse is the same as the adopters; they may just be in a new phase of improvement where the variation in service has increased due to their experimenting with new ideas to improve it.
- The decision to stop doing something new is one that can have a long term impact. Assess why it is that the decision has been made; discuss and help the adopters make their reasoning explicit
- Check whether the issues can be resolved quickly – and do so – or whether they represent more fundamental concerns.

Think about a good idea you have picked up from another person or team and would like to help others adopt similar practices (or just think about a recent guideline that has been sent out).

Are the potential adopters at the pre-contemplative or contemplative stage? Make a few notes about what you can do to help their decision making process.

"Selling" good practice

Whether someone decides to adopt a new idea can be heavily influenced by the way in which they are approached, or the way they tackle the issue. Many early adopters will have to take on the mantle of motivator and encourage their colleagues to adopt the new practices and ideas.

A framework for thinking about the ways in which this can happen is the Tell/Sell/Test/Consult/Co-create model (Senge, 1999).

Telling – what to do, why, when and how
Selling – gaining support for the idea on the basis it fulfils a need
Testing – putting out feelers and seeing what the response is like
Consulting – spending time discussing and debating the issues and the ideas
Co-creating – discovering new ways to understand and solve the problem, together

The impact on individual decision-making is very different according to which approach you might take (see overleaf).

Think about a good idea you have picked up from another person or team and would like to help others adopt similar practices (or just think about a recent guideline that has been sent out).

What approach would you take, and why? Make a few notes:

	Tell	Sell	Test	Consult	Co-create
Motivator	Easy to tell, and can be fooled by the quick decision from adopter even though no action is forthcoming. Disseminating information often falls into this category.	Means an understanding of the target audience and their need is required. Will take more time	Useful when not sure how big the issue is or what the impact of the potential change might be. A way of finding out what stage the potential adopters are at in terms of the change model.	Good idea when the change is going to be significant. Could be too costly and time consuming if the change is predicted to be quite small. If the change is mandated e.g. drug prescribing guidelines, then little point in consulting except for working out any local variations that may be helpful.	Time consuming but probably has the most potential for longer term sustainability, even though it may take longer to achieve any gains (unlikely to get many quick fixes, or early gains with this approach) May take longer to reach the decision to adopt, but the decision will probably hold in the maintenance phase and there is less likelihood of relapse.
Adopter	May feel under pressure and either decide to do something to get the motivator off their case (with no intention of implementing any new ideas), or decide to take more time to do evaluation	Helps the process if the need is obvious. Though participating in benchmarking or other tension for change activities could be painful and off-putting. The motivator's need and your need may be different. Easier to make decisions if linked directly to real needs and requirements.	Difficult to see the point unless it is linked to specific needs. If discussion and debate is available and encouraged then this approach can be useful. Can help adopters arrive at own decisions rather than having them forced upon them.	May require consultation and use it as a means to slow down the decision making process. Effective consultation may help decision's credibility with colleagues who did not participate in the decision making process	If accepting the need for change then this is an effective way to reach decision on what to do when etc. Need to be prepared to spend the time on this. Not all adopters favour this approach due to the time it takes. Many find it easier to take a proposal and then rework it rather than to start from scratch.
Source	May feel embarrassed about others having to adopt the same practices. Could withdraw support that would have helped adopters make decisions	In a good position to understand the adopter's needs. Can help the motivator in understanding how to pitch their communication and manage the process.	Helps if on hand to answer questions raised by both motivator and adopters.	Can provide support by demonstrating how the new ideas can work in practice.	Whilst this step is really about the adopters finding ways to implement new ideas, the source may be helpful in explaining how they arrived at theirs. It may also be a learning opportunity for the source.

Helping the formal decision process

Decisions need not be black or white, yes or no. Where possible it is helpful to approach each adoption decision on the basis that it is a pilot change. The task of those implementing the change is to manipulate it so that it fits their situation. If the change proposed is large, for example installing new patient booking computing systems, then divide the project into smaller stages. This reduces both risk and resistance.

Working with the resistance:

- If an individual or a member of the management team is unwilling to proceed then see whether they will accept a staged implementation, with ongoing review at each step.
- Try to understand their perspective. What can you learn from their point of view?
- Once you've understood their point of view, then find ways to make yours explicit and understandable.
- The patient is often the unifying catalyst in healthcare; focus on the benefits and impact for the patients and carers.

Why should anyone listen to or accept your idea to copy good practice from elsewhere? You will find it helpful to put yourself in the potential adopter's shoes and work out what they feel about the proposed change and what specific barriers they are seeing to making the decision to adopt. How you respond to questions and resistance will reflect on the adopter and a vicious or virtuous cycle may begin (see overleaf).

Summary

The decision-making process is a key step in the adoption of new ideas. Individuals and organisations make decisions in different ways and this can impact the time it takes to actually deliver any results through the implementation of the ideas. Individuals may take longer to decide but tend to implement the practices quicker, whereas organisations can make board decisions quite quickly but it may take many months (if ever) for the changes to be implemented.

There are a variety of tools and techniques that can support the decision-making process. Understanding the stage of change that

The potential adopter says..	You respond by...
"I'm not interested"	• Building rapport and understanding adopter's interests • Finding a focal interest – try the patient's point of view • Listening to other points of view, even if they seem irrelevant
"I have a better idea"	• Acknowledging the idea and then discussing how it might be implemented • Finding the common ground between your ideas • Keeping an open mind; the adopter's may be better
"I'll use this meeting to think through my own problem"	• Ensuring you have the right people involved at the outset • Checking your topic is an important one for the participants • Asking potential adopters for suggestions on how to proceed
"This could impact my work role"	• Acknowledging the potential impact • Presenting the benefits of the change i.e. the relative advantage • Asking for ideas on how to re-invent the good practice to make it more suitable
"I don't want to be involved"	• Finding out why the adopter feels this way • Checking involvement really is necessary • Outlining the importance and benefits of the initiative • Meeting your colleague before any more public meetings

(adapted from Heylin 1991)

a potential adopter is at and then supporting them through the steps can be helpful. At all stages facilitation is important and it helps if the approach taken by the motivators enables adopters' decision-making.

Key points

The stages of change model
• Pre-contemplation
• Contemplation
• Action
• Maintenance
• Relapse

Different approaches that impact on decision-making
• Telling
• Selling
• Testing
• Consulting
• Co-creating

Part 4

Implementing

Section 11

Re-inventing new ways

By the end of this section you will be able to:

- Differentiate between the levels of re-invention required by different types of spread
- Assess the readiness of your target adopters to make the changes
- Use change catalysts to support the adoption of good practice

Adapting knowledge and experience from elsewhere to work in your own environment is a key step in the spread process. Every circumstance and situation is unique. This is why it's so difficult successfully to transfer something that seems to work well in one hospital, to a different hospital.

Without acknowledging this uniqueness and the need therefore to 're-invent' the good practice such that it fits your context, the final implementation stage of the spread process, can founder.

This is one of the paradoxes with the spread and adoption of existing good practice. There are few examples where solutions that worked in one place can be transferred and implemented in their entirety into another place. This can work if the initiative is a brand new one and not one that requires current systems to change in a significant way. In most cases, however, only the essence, the basic concepts of the original good practice are retained, and the solution developed by the adopting individual or team may in fact look quite different from the source.

Why does this re-invention need to occur? Each organisation and team has a unique context with a group of individuals who have their own ideas about what should happen. One of the quickest ways to develop resistance to change is to expect or demand that potential adopters pick up and implement the source's solution in its entirety. There will always be the excuses: "*That won't work here because...*", "*We've done that before and it didn't work...*", "*They had a special...*", "*Our patients are different...*", "*Our management processes are different...*", "*Our IT system means it won't work here...*" etc.

This section starts by checking how the different types of spread (scatter, switch, share and stretch) need different degrees of re-invention. It then includes a technique to assess the readiness of your adopters to change, the concept of change catalysts and how to make them explicit as well as some questions to get the re-invention process started (see opposite).

What changes have you made to your own practice over the last few months? Note down how much re-invention went on as you implemented new ideas from elsewhere:

Different types of spread, different re-invention issues

	Scatter	Switch	Share	Stretch
Definition	Where one simple behaviour or practice is intended to be disseminated to and adopted by very many people	The concept that a good practice from another industry can be implemented in your local context	Sharing of wealth within an organisation by copying practices in one division, unit or group, to others throughout the organisation	Where good practice in a pathway of care is expanded within the organisation, across divisional boundaries as well as across organisational boundaries
Amount of re-invention anticipated	Not much	Significant	Moderate	Fairly large
Issues	• If the idea is small and simple there should not be much re-invention required, especially if the relative advantage is obvious to the adopters. • Many motivators send out complex guidelines and requests for change using the scatter approach when in fact the changes are too complex and are more akin to a share and stretch method.	• Taking a concept from an outside industry requires significant reinvention, not only to test that it really will work, but also to discover a relevant language for the new concepts and ideas.	• Every organisation has pockets of good practice and it seems difficult to get them to spread around. • Competitive concerns, such as vying for resources may play a part in some groups not wishing to share how it is they do what they do. • Within an organisation, there may be a very strong feeling amongst the potential adopters that the source group have some special privileges that help them provide the good practice.	• Crossing boundaries increases the complexity and variability of the process and context. • What works in one part of the pathway is not guaranteed to work further down or up the process. What worked in the hospital may not work in the community setting where there are different priorities and patients tend not to follow steps in the more certain way that happens in hospitals.
What helps	• Making the relative advantage visible and obvious • Keeping the required change very small and simple • Reducing the changes to small parts • Enabling pilots and trials of new ideas	• Must pilot and test first to create own sources of good practice • Extracting the concepts of what works elsewhere and not copying the detailed solutions • Accepting it may not work well in different contexts	• Not pushing the adopters • Helping the source to explain how they manage what they do, in terms the adopters understand. • Not constantly comparing the potential adopters with the source and allowing them to come up with their own solution rather than one that looks like the source's.	• Setting targets and objectives • Helping all members of the pathway to meet and understand how their behaviour impacts on others. • Help wider teams understand the values and principles that helped initiate the original good practice. • Find examples of good practice from other communities.

Assessing the readiness of adopters to change

The Stages of Change Model in the previous section is one of the fundamental assessments you can make about an individual's readiness for change. Another way to analyse readiness is to assess whether the adopters know *WHAT* they need to do and *HOW* to do it. Which of these do you need to work on first with the individual adopter in mind? It is useful to target potential adopters in specific ways that meet their requirements at the time, rather than take a 'one size fits all' approach to spread.

> At a project meeting to improve access to orthopaedic services, each of the four clinicians had a different starting point. Dr A was unclear what needed to be done and certainly wasn't comfortable with knowing how to go about any changes. Dr B had some ideas he had heard from a colleague in another hospital, but didn't know how to implement them. Dr C had recently participated in a redesign project and had ideas on how the changes could be made but was unsure about what the actual goals were for the project. Dr D felt she knew what needed to be done and how to go about it. The project manager felt it would be best to approach each of the clinicians on a one-to-one basis and used the What/How matrix below to assess how best to work with each one.

	Know WHAT to do	Don't know WHAT to do
Know HOW to do it	*Goals and methods to achieve the improvement are familiar* Get on with it! Make sure aims are clear and stakeholders involved. Provide supportive coaching.	*Have method but no goals or detail of what might be useful ideas* Firm up a vision. Challenge understanding of why the change needs to happen. Link performance results to the proposal.
Don't know HOW to do it	*Goals and ideas for change familiar but no clear way to go about it* Spend time understanding the current situation. Gain support of others. Allow the process to evolve and be patient in uncertainty. Celebrate early successes.	*Unsure of the direction* Create dialogue with others. Listen to views and build trust. Seek understanding of current processes and issues. Accept ideas and support from others.

Adapted from Obeng (1997)

Think through a recent experience where you have tried to help
potential adopters re-invent ideas from elsewhere. Did you assume
all adopters were coming from the same starting point? What could
you have done differently?:

Using change catalysts

"A change concept can be said to have the same function as a catalyst. It is a means to start a process. Once the process has started, the catalyst is no longer needed. In the work of improvement,
catalysts are sometimes needed to start the process of creative
thinking. The potential for improvement often lies in coming up
with smarter routines and working procedures, not simply getting people to work harder and faster."

The Federation of Swedish County Councils, 1998

A change catalyst is the essence behind the perceived good practice. For example, when you are
about to overtake another car on the road, then
good practice is to check your rear view mirror. The
catalyst behind this, the idea, is to check the traffic
behind you and to ensure no one else is overtaking
you at the same time. Whilst using rear view mir-
rors is standard good practice, there are other ways
to achieve the same results – some innovative
approaches could be to use a rear view monitor that
displays on your dashboard, have some form of
alarm system, or to stop overtaking under any circumstances! Even for a standard and routine good
practice there are a number of different solutions.

> The National Medicines Management
> Collaborative in the UK has used change
> catalyst to good effect. Following a survey
> of good practice in medicines management
> processes, the project team developed a
> small booklet that summarised each
> example of good practice in only a short
> paragraph. Each example was categorised
> along some themes (catalysts) such as
> communication, co-ordination and review.
> These were highlighted with an example.
> Project teams could find some interesting
> examples and then discuss the ideas
> behind them, using the catalysts. By
> discussing catalysts there was less
> resistance to change and there was no
> compulsion to adopt specific and bespoke
> solutions. Teams were encouraged to make
> changes that would be measurable
> improvements in their local situations.

The important thing when supporting the spread and adoption process, is to separate the solution from the ideas underlying the good practice.

Discovering change catalysts

This is easier when you have more than one example of good practice as this enables you to see the patterns that might exist. However, even if you have only one example, then here are some ways you can go about discovering the underlying concepts.

- Focus on verbs and brainstorm the various actions that seem to be happening in the example of good practice e.g. coordinate, review, communicate, reduce waste, speed up etc.
- Examine the relationships between the people in the process. What do they do and how do they do it?
- Try and explain the good practice as if you were talking to an eight year old! This will force you to simplify and summarise.
- Ask a patient or carer to describe the good practice.
- Avoid any qualifying nouns or descriptions when you write up the change catalysts. For example – "nurse led clinic" is a solution in that it describes the role of the nurse and the means of a clinic. Depending on your example, the catalyst could be "skill upwards" or "enhance role".

Questions to help the re-inventing process
Adapted from Thomas (1997)

If you are encountering a significant amount of resistance to change, then you might need to set aside some time to review what it is you are trying to spread and help other adopt. As mentioned previously, one of the main causes of resistance is pushing solutions on adopters. One way to avoid this is to spend time assessing how the solutions and ideas from elsewhere can be re-invented to suit the local circumstances. Rather than defending the solution, be proactive and open the solution and new ideas up for further debate.

- What could we change to make this work better?
- How can we modify the structure or the roles?
- How can the scope and scale be changed?
- How can the practice be simplified?

- How can we change a weakness into a strength?
- What can be eliminated?
- What can be rearranged?
- What can be swapped around?
- What other uses could this have?

Do it now!

Turn the time you would spend on developing lists of tasks and prioritising them, into action. Re-invention is an active step.

Summary

Whilst re-invention sounds like the opposite to spreading good practice, the important factor is to re-invent where there are already ideas to make an improvement. David Fillingham (Modernisation Agency Director, National Health Service) uses the term "*assisted wheel re-invention*" to make this clear. There are many ideas out there, so pick some useful ones and try to deliver improvements by adapting these to suit your local circumstance.

Key points

Different types of spread have different re-invention issues
- Scatter: not much re-invention is necessary
- Switch: significant re-invention required
- Share: moderate re-invention
- Stretch: fairly large amounts of local adjustment needed

Adopters differ according to whether they know *WHAT* to do and *HOW* to do it:
- Know what and how – get on with it
- Know what but not how – provide support for change
- Know how but not what – work on goals and ideas
- Don't know how or what – start by working on vision, goals and ideas. Build on current processes.

Focus on and spread change catalysts and ideas, not solutions

Section 12

Unlearning old ways

By the end of this section you will be able to:

- Explain why unlearning is important
- Apply ideas to help the unlearning process
- Describe ways to reduce resistance to giving up old ways

The first step in unlearning is to recognise the practices that need to be forgotten, replaced or changed. This is not as easy as it may sound since what many people think and describe as their actions is often very different from what they actually do. The next issue for working with individuals is the nature of expertise and success. The greater the specialism and achievement, then usually fewer mistakes are made and there is thus less opportunity for learning. Add to this the high investment in working years to develop a set of practices. Not many experts enjoy relinquishing or risking behaviours that seemed to have worked well for them so far.

Finally, when working with organisations we are surrounded by the stories of long forgotten practices and improvement efforts. One way to deal with this cultural resistance to the adoption of new ideas is to generate new stories, building on what works well now.

What you say you do, is probably different from what you actually do!

Implementing good practice requires you to see things in a different way; to unlearn what you have done before, and to do it a new way.

This is particularly difficult when you are not aware that your actions do not match your explanations of what you do.

Further reading
Chris Argyris (1998)
Teaching Smart People to
Learn in *Harvard
Business Review*, On
knowledge management,
Boston, USA

This is a well-known phenomena; look for it in your organisation, with teams and individuals, and recognise that it is an important part of what you might perceive to be resistance to change.

> A general physician is given the role of clinical director for the medical directorate in an acute trust.
>
> He has always been a proponent of teamwork and now he has completed his MBA he has a greater understanding of the theories and methodologies. He uses the directorate meetings as a means of highlighting the importance of working appropriately in multi-disciplinary teams.
>
> However, his general manager, who is working with him on a specific improvement project, notices that whenever he is working in his own multi-disciplinary team, he displays little evidence of using his theories. Two of his team have complained to you about the lack of teamwork that they perceive may impact on patient care.
>
> The physician is not aware of this conflict between what he is saying and what he is doing. Argyris (1978) suggests his 'theory-in-use' is not the same as his 'espoused theory'. This is common.

To help teams and individuals work through this issue you can:

- Use techniques such as process mapping or audit, to demonstrate what actually happens rather than what people perceive happens.
- Observe, using an independent facilitator if necessary, the current practice and feed back to the participants the view of what is actually happening
- Ask people involved what they perceive are the gaps between others behaviour and what they say they do (individuals can often see it in others, if not themselves)
- Dedicate time at project meetings to discuss and reflect on the issue

One of the behaviours that is often perceived as resistance to change and unlearning is seen in comments such as "*I already do that...*", "*We do something similar...*", "*What we do isn't a problem...*". Without helping practitioners and managers see what is actually happening, it is easy to reach a stalemate in the spread and adoption process.

Specialism and success can hinder unlearning

Expertise is not always a good thing. When it comes to spreading good practice it can be a barrier. A niche is often a dead-end. A specialist may have a lot to lose in terms of both economic and social status should the job role change significantly. What you know and believe in is part of the unconscious resistance we all feel when faced with new ideas.

Professionals are experts usually in a specialist area. Because of this expertise you may not be used to experiencing failure. This makes it more difficult to learn, and to unlearn. When faced with difficulties you may unconsciously become defensive – it's a way of thinking that just happens. You may not be used to having your reasoning processes questioned. So now you have become resistant to the idea of changing, mostly unwittingly and unconsciously.

Many experts don't notice technical advances in their field. As part of developing specialist skills you have developed filters and tend to connect with only a very small amount of information that you perceive to be relevant. You've developed habits, reflexes, good and bad practices, many of which are not under your conscious control. Like driving a car. This unconscious behaviour is a necessary part of how you work (or else the brain would become overwhelmed) and it is these deep processes that are often at the root of the difficulty some people have in unlearning old ways and adopting new behaviours.

Ideas to assist unlearning

1 Bring in a stranger and ask for their views on the current and proposed practice. Often they will see unusual aspects of the problem and their comments can be revealing.
2 Accept and analyse all dissenting opinions, they have validity. Organisational structures and hierarchies can block protests. You are best able to move forward if you have insight into others' views.
3 Magnify dissatisfaction. If some practitioners and managers are dissatisfied with the current practice, then use this to help them change.
4 Leverage surprises. If something unusual happens then investigate what and why it happened. Is there something in here that will support the change process?

5 Try out small changes and experiment. This will reduce the risk of large change and enable experts to alter their behaviour incrementally.

Note a recent example where you perceive you may have been resistant to change.

What would have helped you unlearn your 'old ways'?

So far we have concentrated on helping individuals unlearn. However, the context within which they work is an important factor that you also need to take into account when planning and implementing your spread activities.

One way to start understanding what cultural behaviours are entrenched in the organisation is to examine how good ideas get rejected. This may shed insight into what happens in the decision making process and the mental models of those involved.

Myths and legends

All organisations have stories as part of their cultural structure. These may be rooted in actual events but are likely to have adapted over time. If these tales exist in the area where you are implementing new practices, then they will need your understanding, interest and attention. It is usually an informal leadership and communication structure that generates and sustains such stories. This 'underground' network is valuable in the unlearning and change process.

Actions you can take:

- Discover relevant stories by seeking out opinion leaders or by asking new employees what they've heard
- Work through the story and analyse how it might be a barrier to unlearning
- Discuss your findings with staff
- Help create new stories by shedding light on the good things that work well and sharing the stories of how they came about.

Reducing resistance

You can never assume that other people are as excited about the new idea as you. Many of your colleagues will see only the difficulties. Remember there is an unlearning process that you will all need to go through.

Checklist for opinion leaders and motivators

- ❏ Demonstrate your personal commitment to the new ideas
- ❏ Assess others' commitment
- ❏ Discover reasons for resistance
- ❏ Remove or work with barriers
- ❏ Offer support and encouragement throughout the change process
- ❏ Provide as much relevant information as possible
- ❏ Involve people in ways that help them show commitment
- ❏ Negotiate expectations
- ❏ Recognise the phases of denial, anger, action, then acceptance, that most individuals and teams go through when experiencing change

Summary

The unlearning process is often forgotten in the haste to encourage adopters to take on new ideas and behaviours. By focusing on the current behaviours, making them explicit and obvious to the adopter, you can support the change process in a constructive way.

Key points

Espoused theory (what we say) is often very different from theory-in-action (what we actually do). Taking note of the difference and making the actual behaviour more explicit is helpful in the change process.

Assist unlearning by:

- Bringing in a stranger to observe and feedback
- Accepting and analysing all dissenting opinions
- Magnifying dissatisfaction
- Leveraging surprises
- Experimenting with small changes

Part 5

Putting it together

Section 13

Monitoring progress

By the end of this section you will be able to:

- Design a process to monitor the spread and adoption of good ideas
- Explain why measuring awareness of the tension for change and of good ideas is crucial to measuring your progress
- Describe some ways to recover from 'failure'

Organisations spend substantial amounts of money attempting to spread pilot project results to other parts of the organisation with the aim of achieving similar benefits elsewhere. Just because the practice you are encouraging others to adopt worked in another organisation, for another team, is no guarantee that it will work in the new place. Without a system to check your progress you will never be sure that your efforts have been worthwhile. These spread projects are often unique in they're one of the few areas of substantial spending where monitoring of the progress does not happen. One of the reasons for this is the difficulty in working out what should be monitored and by whom.

Working in the social system means it is often difficult to separate out the adoption of new ideas in a busy workplace. Drawing attention to the issues might be helpful in some cases, and not in others. You can focus on monitoring when the solution is adopted, though this is difficult to recognise if there is significant reinvention. Alternatively, you can focus on the underlying performance that you're trying to improve; this is a good way to measure, especially if you have a number of initiatives underway in the same area at the same time.

The pilot projects to improve access to primary care had been very successful and the CEO was keen to spread the results from the initial three practices to the remaining twelve practices in the group. The pilot projects had taken two years to deliver their achievements and the projects had run fairly standalone and in isolation for the remaining practices.

The fact the target practices for adoption had not heard of the projects slowed down the whole of the spread phase. The project manager had to start from scratch, selling the ideas and helping the practices discover the need for change. She felt this slowed the momentum for the change and even impacted on the sustainability of results at the pilot practices.

"If I'd spent more time raising awareness of the issue and the good ideas with the non-pilot practices they would have been more ready for change. They would probably have also supported sustainability, as there would have been a good system of feedback and confirmation about the results; the pilots would feel more confident if they saw others adopting their ideas more quickly. It's no good chasing implementation when people haven't even made the decision to change, or even worse, don't even see the need!"

How do you know what's happening in your system?

Whatever your strategy, the most important factor is you have a measurement strategy. By monitoring what is going on you will have developed a feedback system that will help you learn about how your system changes. The graphs and measurements will provide you with a window on the systems you are working with, showing what is working and what might need more support and attention.

This section will describe a method for monitoring the process of spread and adoption of new ideas. One useful method of monitoring progress and finding ways to leverage change is to separate out three key steps in the adoption process:

1 **Awareness**; what is the awareness level of the adopters. Do they know about the innovation? How much do they know? Are they aware even of the need for change?
2 **Decision making**; when did the adopters make the decision to implement the new ideas?
3 **Implementation**; has the new practice been implemented? To what extent?

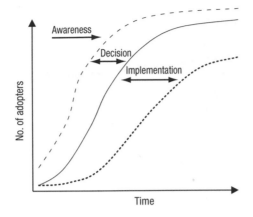

The 'S-curve' shows how the cumulative number of adopters increases over time.

At first the communication efforts help potential adopters become aware of the new ideas. The next step is for them to make the decision whether to adopt or not. A useful point of leverage for change is to find ways to support this decision making process.

The final step is the implementation of the new ideas. This can take a while longer than the initial step of gaining awareness.

Spread plans need to take these timing differences into account.

Awareness

Communication and awareness is key to the adoption process. Any programme of spread needs to focus on a multi-method strategy of increasing potential adopters' awareness of the benefits and details of the proposed new ideas and practices. The message and the way in which it is delivered will have an impact on the attitude an adopter has about the new practice and this will impact the decision making process.

There are two basic measurements for awareness:

1 The need for change
2 The good ideas

The need for change

This links back to the Model of Change discussed in section 10. Unless the potential adopters are aware of the need to alter their behaviour, then you will most likely encounter significant resistance to change.

One of the simplest ways to measure this form of awareness is to use your own perceptions and judgements, following discussions with the potential adopters. Alternatively you could ask them to complete a simple questionnaire, though this may, in itself, generate some resistance to change or impact commitment to the issue.

The good ideas

This links back to change catalysts and the reinvention of good practice from elsewhere into the local context (Section 11). Use the WHAT/HOW – KNOW/DON'T KNOW matrix to identify whether the problem is one of not knowing enough of the WHAT. You can discover this by asking questions and engaging in dialogue with the potential adopters. Again, if you encounter resistance or lack of awareness of good ideas, it may be because you are pushing a set solution that doesn't, in the mind of the adopters, solve their problems.

These measurements are for the purpose of learning as well as providing some management information. It is not the intent to apply scientific rigour or to conduct a research project. This is about helping others change their behaviours and you finding ways to asses whether the methods you are using are being effective or not. You are seeking feedback as early as possible to confirm whether your actions are constructive, supportive and effective.

Think about the target adopters for a specific good practice that you have in mind? Note down how you would test their awareness of the need for change and the good ideas to solve the problems?

Some questions for measuring awareness

- Against a baseline, who is now more aware than they were before the communications programme started?
- Are some groups and professions gaining awareness quicker than others? Does this matter?
- Do the opinion leaders know about the new practices? Are their views positive?
- Which of the communications methods (e.g. video, seminar, article) had the most impact in terms of raising awareness?
- Is awareness dropping off or increasing over time?
- Which part of the message or which method seems to have the least impact or create resistance to change?
- What does the pattern of awareness look like? What can you learn from this?
- What is the slope of the curve? How quickly is awareness increasing? What can you do to speed it up?
- Are the target adopters covered in the measurements? Has any group been left out? Is the span of population wide enough to generate momentum for change?

Decision-making

Where the adopters are relatively autonomous and can make their own decisions, implementation can happen quite quickly. In organisations where the decisions are made by a central management team, it can take much longer to actually achieve implementation.

A general surgeon had heard from a colleague in another hospital about the new way of booking patients for operations and immediately made the decision to do the same, as he felt it was good for his patients. Unfortunately, he had difficulty in gaining support for the changes as it meant some modifications to the computer booking system. The decision to change was quick, but the implementation took a long time.

He thought this interesting as he sat on the board of the hospital in his capacity as medical director. There he often participated in a decision making process that seemed to take months to get even the simplest things agreed. Yet, many times, the decisions were acted upon by staff far more quickly than in the case of his personal decision.

He spent time reflecting on the importance of organisational decision making and how important it was to support individuals who are trying to deliver improvements in their own practice.

Some questions for measuring decision-making

- Who needs to make the decision for the new ideas and practices to be adopted? Why?
- Who has made the decision to adopt the new ideas and to change their practice?
- What is the threshold for someone to decide to make a change? What can be done to help the adopter over this barrier?
- Has the decision been made to adopt all the new ideas, or just part of the system being spread? And why?
- What is their reason for making the decision?
- When did they make the decision?
- What or who influenced their decision-making?
- What is stopping a decision being made?
- Which opinion leaders influence the target group of adopters?
- What does the pattern of decision-making look like? What can we learn from this?
- What can you do to influence the decision-making process? Are you targeting the most appropriate decision makers?

Implementation

At some stage you need to know when the changes have been made and to check whether they are having the desired outcome.

The Primary Care Collaborative (UK NHS) measures include:

Project outcome: The % of patients prescribed aspirin (CHD aim)

Proxy: The 3rd available appointment to see a GP (Access aim)

The project outcome

You can use a measurement to test whether the changes are having the desired effect. This is one of the best methods as it is directly linked to the purpose behind the spread of good practice – to deliver improvement.

The proxy

This is a measurement that provides information about the wider aim or purpose of the changes. It is a useful alternative when measuring outcomes is too complicated or the results won't be seen in a short to medium time frame.

The solution

It is very tempting to measure the number of times the solution has been copied. Of course this depends on the amount of re-invention that take place. At what stage is your solution still the same solution? How can you tell if the solution is having the desired positive benefits? Apart from these fundamental questions, we return to the original difficulty of spreading solutions – they don't spread, ideas do. If you put in place measurements to count solutions then you may create resistance to change and slow up the improvement process.

Some questions for measuring implementation

- Have new behaviours been implemented?
- Are you seeing the improved results you expected to see?
- Are the results and benefits similar to those achieved by the pilot projects?
- Have all the parts of the new practice been implemented, or just bits of it? And why?
- Do the adopters feel they made the right decision? What are the implications of this?
- What messages, and in what way, are the new adopters sharing their experiences with others?
- What influenced the implementation that was not part of the formal communication and project activities?
- To what extent was the innovation adapted by the adopters? What might this mean for future plans for spread and communication?

Call to mind the good ideas you are trying to help others adopt. Note down the specific measurements that are important to your organisation or profession

Developing your own measurement strategy

This needs to reflect the specific goals and aim of your spread project. You might need to take into account:

a) Organisational goals
b) Requirements from other statutory and non-statutory bodies
c) Requests from funders/stakeholders for feedback on progress
d) Profession specific requirements
e) Recent audits or other local investigations
f) Availability of information systems
g) Ease of data collection and management
h) Availability of target adopters for discussion and dialogue
i) Acceptance of a level of measurement aimed at learning rather than research

As with many change processes, designing strategies in the back room is seldom rewarding or effective. The best way to begin measuring your progress is to start with one measurement and learn from it. Keep it simple and try to collect data that gives you feedback over time so that you can see how your efforts are making an impact.

Dealing with 'failure'

Some of your efforts won't work out as planned. Treat them as learning experiences. If you have useful monitoring systems, you will be able to learn and adjust your plans as your project progresses.

- Don't give up if it seems not to be working. Be creative in working round the problem and keep trying
- Allow failure by not blaming anyone for the difficulties. Get all those involved to work through how to fix the problem. Use your data to help you understand what is going on, and not going on. Collect more data if that will be useful.
- Analyse what went wrong and what you will do differently next time.
- Let your peers know about your difficulties and help them avoid making the same mistakes

Summary

A monitoring system means you have a window through which to observe and gain insight about how your system adopts new behaviours. It is useful to keep an eye on awareness levels, decision-making processes as well as the implementation of good ideas. Using measurement means you never really experience failure – you just have many opportunities for learning.

Key points

Measure
- Awareness
- Decision-making
- Implementation

Section 14

Planning a spread activity

By the end of this section you will be able to:

- Prioritise your efforts
- Create an overall implementation strategy
- Use a flexible planning system
- Design an appropriate infrastructure

The introduction to this workbook declared there was no specific model or framework for spreading good practice. The reasoning behind this is the importance of context and community. Each target team or organisation has its own specific circumstances influencing the way they behave and the rate at which they will, or will not, adopt new behaviours.

The social system, both shadow and formal, is a fundamental feature of how new behaviours are adopted. Because you are dealing with individuals, all of whom have their own motivations, and because each time they interact with each other they create their context, it is difficult to produce a master plan for your spread activities. However, you can spend time prioritising and targeting your efforts, drawing up an overall strategy and then using a flexible planning system to keep track of progress.

This section will draw on and reference tools and techniques from other sections in this workbook. Your planning tasks as described in this section include:

- Analysis and preparation
- Prioritising your activities
- Creating a plan
- Building an infrastructure

Analysis and preparation

This is a key stage and one that is often disregarded.

> You have just been appointed as the project manager responsible for ensuring that the results of a pilot project creating one-stop access clinics for cancer diagnosis from one hospital are spread throughout a network of twelve hospitals.
>
> When you checked with a project manager doing a similar task in another area you discovered that she went straight to action and tried to get changes made in a very short time. Your assessment is that this strategy didn't work very well. Your instinct is to do a lot more planning and analysis, listening to what people say and developing your understanding about how the individuals and teams in your system learn.

You need to assess and analyse:

- The drivers for change and stakeholder requirements (Section 13)
- Your target adopters (Section 7)
- The type of good practice you are dealing with; scatter, switch, stretch, share (Section 5)
- The best way to describe the good practice (Section 6)
- The change catalysts, the good ideas underlying the good practice (Section 11)

A good planning step is to document your assessment using the points above and then discuss your findings with colleagues and stakeholders. You may find you have been given targets and deadlines that make the assumption that this analysis has already been done. It is useful to carry this assessment out again yourself, even over a day or two, as it forms an important part of developing your own understanding of what it is you are required to achieve.

Prioritising your activities

Do you try to carry out all the tasks required of you? Make some notes about how you prioritise your work.

Based on your analyses you will need to decide which tasks to do first. There are three factors to think about here:

1 Elapsed time and actual time
2 Dependencies
3 Impact

Elapsed time and actual time

Actual time is the amount of time taken on a task whilst elapsed time covers the actual time plus time spent waiting for responses or for something else to happen that may not be related to the project. Many spread projects underestimate the amount of elapsed time that social systems take to absorb and integrate messages about new ideas. This links to the importance of measuring awareness (Section 13).

Dependencies

It is important to identify activities and steps that cannot proceed until something else has been done. These dependencies may be an integral part of the good practice you are trying to spread. It is these dependencies that result in long lead times and they need to be worked on early in your programme.

A *dependency*.

You can't expect secretaries to use a new e-mail based booking system unless they already have access to e-mail and are confident users.

Impact

Gaining wins early on in the process is always useful. Though be sure to avoid targeting the innovators of your adopter group (Section 7). It is often better to target those areas first that will have high impact on the overall outcome of your efforts.

	Easy to accomplish	Difficult to accomplish
High impact on patient care	Priority	Assess – do next?
Low impact on patient care	Do if need a success	Hold off

One way of using the matrix above is to enter all the tasks and activities you think need to be accomplished, into the appropriate boxes. Then use this as the basis of discussion with your stakeholders and the target adopters. You will find this a useful way to make explicit various motivations for change that you can use later when helping others implement the actual changes.

Creating a plan

A spread plan is not like a plan to build a new ward. As adoption and change is a personal transition where the social and shadow system is very important, you need a planning system that is flexible and dynamic. One that can provide you with an overall picture on your progress and hint at where to direct your efforts, rather than a plan you slavishly follow step by step in a linear way. Spread projects need to be able to move with the ebb and flow of the communities within which they are working, and the planning system needs to recognise this.

You can design your own planning system. There are three techniques that you might find useful:

1 SMART goals
2 "Who is doing what" matrix
3 Completeness and coverage matrix

SMART goals

Your plan will need a set of aims or goals that clearly describe what you intend to achieve. These should be:

- **S**pecific
- **M**easurable
- **A**chievable
- **R**ealistic
- **T**ime-based

Your implementation activity needs a clear focus.

- Is the change targeted in an area where small changes will deliver large improvements?
- Are the aims of the improvement clear enough to help adopters capture and transfer the right practices?
- Do the aims provide guidance for re-invention?

"Who is doing what" matrix

This assessment focuses on the roles people need to play at different stages in the spread programme. You can start by drafting your thoughts in the matrix and then sharing it with colleagues for discussion. Make notes as you progress on your project. You may find this matrix organises your learning and helps you target areas for particular effort.

The matrix has some guidance notes in it. These are to get you started and are by no mans a complete list of the types of activities that can happen at each stage for each role. If you are unsure about the roles then check back to section 4.

	Motivator	Source	Adopter
Identify the type of spread (Section 5)	Scatter, share, switch, stretch?	Where did the idea come from?	Which one will work best in this community and context?
Describe the good practice and ideas (Section 6)	Use the factors described in Section 6.	Involve and help them elicit change catalysts (Section 11)	Use language the adopters recognise.
Target the adopters (Section 7)	At all levels; organisational, group, individual	Assess target plans	Decide who is appropriate to start changing first
Communicate (Section 8)	Key awareness driving activities.	Key role in providing demonstration, explanation and support.	Learn to be good receivers.
Matching the opportunity to the gap (Section 9)	Audit and other activities		Make own behaviour explicit (Section 12)
Deciding whether to adopt or reject (Section 10)	Support and monitor decision-making	Provide support	Commit to change
Re-inventing new ways (Section 11)	Develop capability for redesign and creative thinking. Don't force solutions.	Avoid pushing own solutions or criticising modifications	Apply creative thinking
Unlearning old ways (Section 12)	Help make behaviours explicit		Help make behaviours explicit
Monitoring progress (Section 13)	Check, monitor and provide feedback	Support	Provide feedback
Planning (Section 14)	Renew and update planning system		Engage in providing data and information for the period of the project

Completeness and coverage matrix

A key part of your planning system is to be able to agree and then keep track on who is expected to adopt which parts of the good practice. Many spread projects include a number of elements that the adopters are required to take on. Different groups will take these on at different times and in different orders. Requiring everyone to do the same thing at the same time across a number of different organistions is an unreasonable expectation of yourself and of them!

Remember the strength of the social system in your spread plan. You can use the hierarchical systems, though they are limited. The purpose of your planning system is to keep track of what is actually happening, and to direct your efforts to where they can be best employed.

The chart below is an example of a flipchart marked out showing the different organisations across the top (1 to 5) and the various parts of the good practice (down the left hand column). Notes were made on the chart using different coloured sticky notes. On the notes was up to date information about the status of the activities going on in the specific organisation.

Monitoring implementation

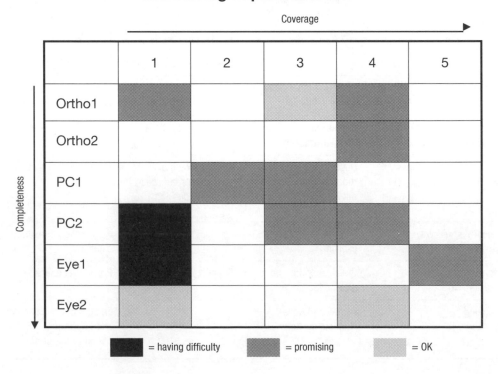

In the previous example, coverage applies to five different hospitals and completeness refers to the various changes that need to be implemented in the various clinics to achieve the access objectives.

The colour coding used on the plan is an indication of the current state of progress. Often, with little explanation, some changes are adopted quickly, whilst one area that was going well has setbacks. You will also notice that this system enables you to see where you do not know what is happening and therefore where you might like to spend a little time (as shown by the blanks).

Building an infrastructure

Some spread projects are quite small and informal activities whereas some can be large, formal activities with resources commensurate with the stakeholder expectations.

Make some notes what sort of infrastructure you think you'll need to implement your spread project.

There are three types of infrastructure

1 Hard – buildings, office space, computers etc.
2 People – project managers, administrative support etc.
3 Variable – supplies, money for locums, meeting room hire etc.

Your infrastructure needs to reflect the specific circumstances of your local community, the expectations of your stakeholders and the available funding.

Questions to think about when developing your infrastructure

- What is available that can be tapped into; such as existing audit facilitators, organisational development work?
- Who is expected to pay for the cost of implementing the solution? Will this be borne directly by the adopting groups and organisations?
- How many project managers will be required? How is this balanced against the need to free up adopters to make their own changes?
- Will locums be required? What is their availability? Is there sufficient funding?
- How will you bring the community together? Will adopters be expected to visit the source of good practice or vice versa?
- What communication techniques do you think would be most appropriate? Is there the funding and the infrastructure (e.g. e-mail) to support this?

Summary

There is no specific formula for planning a spread activity or programme. There are some techniques to help you, but the most important factor is that you design an infrastructure and approach that is best suited to the community within which you are working.

Key points

Key tasks
- Analysis and preparation
- Prioritising your activities
- Creating a plan
- Building an infrastructure

Creating a plan
- SMART goals
- "Who is doing what" matrix
- Coverage and completeness matrix

Types of infrastructure
- Hard
- People
- Variable

Bibliography

Argyris, C. (1998) 'Teaching Smart People to Learn' in *Harvard Business Review*, On knowledge management, Boston, USA

Argyris, C. & Schon, D. (1978) *Organizational Learning: a Theory of Action Perspective.* Addison-Wesley, Reading MA

Charney, C., (1994) *The Instant Manager.* Kogan Page, UK

Fraser (a), S.W. 'Spreading good practice; how to prepare the ground', *Health Management*, June 2000

Fraser (b), S.W. 'Spread good practice by stepping in my shoes, not treading on my toes', *The Systems Thinker*, Vol.11 No.8, October 2000.

Garvin, D. (1998) 'Building a learning organisation' in *Harvard Business Review*, On knowledge management. Boston, USA

Granovetter, M. (1973) 'The strength of weak ties', *American Journal of Sociology*, 78, 1360–1380

Gross, N., Giacquinta, J.B. & Bernstein, M. (1971) *Implementing Organisational Innovations; A Sociological Analysis of Planned Educational Change.* Harper International, New York

Hersey, P. & Blanchard, K. (1988) *Management of Organisational Behaviour: Utilizing Human Resources* (5th ed.). Englewood Cliffs, NJ: Prentice-Hall

Heylin, A. (1991) *Putting it Across: The Art of Communicating, Persuading and Presenting.* Duncan Petersen Publishing, London

Hurwitz, B. (1998) *Clinical Guidelines and the Law.* Radcliffe Medical Press. UK

Hutton, P. (1988) *Survey Research for Managers.* Macmillan, Basingstoke.

Obeng, E. (1997) *New Rules for the New World.* Capstone, UK

O'Dell, C. & Grayson, C. (1998) *If Only We Knew What We Know.* The Free Press, USA

Prochaska, J. & DiClemente, C. (1984) *The Transtheoretical Approach: Crossing Traditional Boundaries of Therapy*, Daw-Jones Irwin.

Robbins, H. & Finley, M. (1998) *Why Change Doesn't Work.* Orion, UK

Rogers, E. (1995) *The Diffusion of Innovations.* The Free Press, USA

Senge, P. (1999) *The Dance of Change.* Nicholas Brearley, UK

Smith, P.R. (1996) *Marketing Communications. An Integrated Approach.* Kogan Page, London

The Federation of Swedish County Councils, Genombrott (1998) *Reducing Queues and Waiting Times to and Within Health Care.* Enskede Offset AB Stockholm

Thresher, B. & Biggin, J. (1993) *Manage the Message.* Century Business, UK

Torrington, D. & Hall, L. (1987) *Personnel Management: A New Approach.* Prentice-Hall, Herts

Valente, T.W. (1999) *Network Models of the Diffusion of Innovations.* Hampton Press Inc, New Jersey

Westphal, J.D., Gulati, R. & Shortell, S.M. (1997) Customisations or conformity? An institutional and network perspective on the content and consequences of TQM adoption. *Administrative Science Quarterly*, 42: 366–394

Zaltman & Duncan (1977) *Strategies for Planned Change.* Wiley, New York